The Playboater's Handbook II

More Great DVDs from Fox Chapel Publishing

**Filleting Fish -
Freshwater DVD**
ISBN: 978-1-896980-65-2 **$14.95**

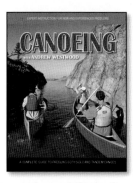

**Canoeing with Andrew
Westwood DVD**
ISBN: 978-1-56523-657-8 **$19.95**

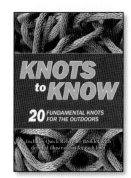

Knots to Know DVD
978-1-896980-55-3 **$14.95**

**Playboating with
Ken Whiting DVD**
ISBN: 978-1-896980-63-8 **$29.95**

**Recreational Kayaking
The Essential Skills
and Safety DVD**
ISBN: 978-1-56523-660-8 **$19.95**

**Whitewater Kayaking
with Ken Whiting DVD**
ISBN: 978-1-56523-664-6 **$29.95**

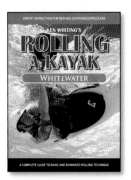

**Rolling a Kayak -
Whitewater DVD**
ISBN: 978-1-56523-658-5 **$26.95**

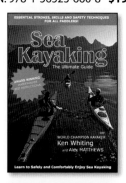

**Sea Kayaking: The
Ultimate Guide DVD**
ISBN: 978-1-56523-663-9 **$29.95**

b.EAST DVD
ISBN: 978-1-56523-662-2 **$19.95**

Look for These DVDs at Your Local Bookstore or Specialty Retailer or at *www.FoxChapelPublishing.com*

Ken Whiting

THE PLAYBOATER'S HANDBOOK II

The Ultimate Guide to Freestyle Kayaking

Photos by Paul Villecourt

THE HELICONIA PRESS

an Imprint of Fox Chapel Publishing
www.FoxChapelPublishing.com

© 2002 by Ken Whiting

Written by: Ken Whiting
Photography by: Paul Villecourt, with additional photos by Rob Faubert, Ruth Gordon, Dan Campbell, Lauren Gervais, and Dale Jardine
Design and Layout: Ken Whiting

ISBN 978-1-896980-74-4

To learn more about the other great books from Fox Chapel Publishing, or to find a retailer near you, call toll-free 800-457-9112 or visit us at *www.FoxChapelPublishing.com*.

Note to Authors: We are always looking for talented authors to write new books. Please send a brief letter describing your idea to Acquisition Editor, 1970 Broad Street, East Petersburg, PA 17520.

Printed in China
First printing

Playboating is an activity with inherent risks, and this book is designed as a general guide, not a substitute for formal, professional instruction. The publisher and the author do not take responsibility for the use of any of the materials or methods described in this book. By following any of the procedures described within, you do so at your own risk.

CONTENTS

Flatwater and Eddyline Moves

Wave Moves

Hole Moves

River Moves

There are so many people to thank who in one way or another have allowed me not only to publish this book, but also to pursue my dreams… In particular, I thank my best friend and loving partner, Nicole, my incredibly supportive parents, and my brother Jeff and Yas. The unending support, patience and encouragement you guys have shown me has been invaluable and so much appreciated. I also want to thank my greatest friends and partners, Kevin Varette, James McBeath and Chad Hitchins. You guys keep me energized and excited about everything I do.

A big thanks to the gang on the Ottawa River, who have fueled my passion for the sport and are in themselves one of the reasons that I do what I do.

To Paul Villecourt, who puts his heart into his magnificent photography, which has helped to make this book what it is.

A special thanks to my Grandmother, Cindy Jamieson, Corran Addison, Steve Fisher, Tyler Curtis, EJ, Eugene Buchanan, Ruth Gordon, Rob Faubert, Craig Langford, Billy Harris, Brendan Mark, Lauren Gervais, Lee Gagne, all my sponsors, and everyone else who has allowed me to follow my dreams, while at the same time making the journey so enjoyable.

INTRODUCTION

So many things have changed within the whitewater paddling industry over the past 10 years. Most notable is the number of boat designs popping up each year. There are so many new boats that one needs to make a concerted effort to stay on top of it all. Then there's the remarkable evolution of the pro-boater. Once, only a handful of paddling gods sacrificed everything for their whitewater passion and pushed the sport to new levels. It seems these fabled beings have multiplied and evolved into what we call 'pro-boaters'. These pro-boaters have popped up in virtually every local paddling community and have helped drive the sport of whitewater kayaking to unprecedented levels.

Whether you like these changes or not, you need to accept them because the reality is that whitewater kayaking has changed for good. No longer is it an activity exclusive to the hardcore outdoor enthusiast who looks to test his or her own resolve against the awesome and unpredictable powers of Mother Nature. Whitewater paddling is quickly becoming recognized as a sport for anyone with an interest in the outdoors and adventure. A huge part of this gravitation towards the mainstream is due to the growth of freestyle kayaking and the consequent efforts of boat designers to create the most playful, user-friendly, whitewater crafts possible. Freestyle kayaks are so user-friendly that novice paddlers will often find themselves bouncing and spinning on waves before they know how to competently front surf! But, as amazing as the equipment has become, it will take a paddler only so far on its own. There comes a time when proper techniques need to be applied in order to get the utmost from your kayak, and that's what this book is about.

I wrote 'The Playboater's Handbook II' with a few goals in mind. I wanted to clearly explain and demonstrate how every playboating move is performed, without the time constraints of a video. I also wanted to introduce an essential set of skills and concepts that provide the foundation for every current playboating move and for every new playboating move that will pop up.

With that said, this book will take you only so far. Once you have a clear idea of what needs to be done, it's up to you to hit the water and play as hard as you can. When you get stuck on a move, ask someone! When you get frustrated with a play spot, watch how the best boaters are dealing with it. It is no secret that the most successful people in the world have taken other people's good ideas and built on them. Take any opportunities to do the same on and off the river and I know you'll reach the goals that you set for yourself. In the end, though reaching your goals is gratifying, it is the journey there that keeps drawing us back to the river. I can only hope that your personal playboating journey is as enjoyable and as life-changing as mine has been.

FOREWORD – CORRAN ADDISON

"To air is human; to land it, divine." I wish this to be my epitaph.

Since my early days of kayaking, I have regarded the aerial moves of other sports in awe. In fact, as early as 1983, while sitting on a beach in Durban, South Africa, I witnessed boogie boarders launching off the lips of waves, and performing the most fascinating moves imaginable.

It was to be almost 10 years before I would begin to tap into this with a kayak. Admittedly, I am at fault. Had my eyes been opened to the possibilities earlier, or my own feeble abilities been greater, then I would have made the breakthrough much sooner.

But I am weak. I succumbed easily to the pressures and opinions and prejudices of those around me, those in the know that made it quite clear that we would never reach such heights in a kayak. And why shouldn't they be right? After all, I was some young whippersnapper from Africa; penniless, and in awe of all that was American. I was in the company of proven athletes, those in the know that had climbed through the ranks to become the best that kayaking had to offer, and they said it couldn't be done. And besides, I have a funny accent, so that automatically excludes any opinion I might have.

How many times did I hear "we have learned all there is to know about kayaking; all that is left is to perfect it"? How true this was about kayaking in the last part of the 20th century, and the onus of responsibility for this short sightedness falls equally upon me for not being more opinionated about what deep down, I knew to be possible.

Only two years ago there were less than a dozen paddlers in the world who could air their kayak on a regular basis. Both designers and paddlers are to blame for this tardy advancement. As one who believes, and always has believed deep down, that aerial moves are not only possible in a kayak, but potentially the most magnificent, most spectacular of all water sports, I am to blame more than any for not pushing sooner, harder and with more conviction.

For this, I ask forgiveness from the kayaking world, for though I was certainly responsible for directing and working with a fantastic group of paddlers in developing the base concepts in equipment and technique that has enabled the universal development and exploration into aerial acrobatics, I more than any had the tools, the means and the abilities to have progressed faster. As the designer for Riot, a company that I own in part, I had to convince no one but myself that what I was doing was right or wrong. My peers have their investors, bosses and boards of directors to answer to. I have only myself, so my sin is greater than any. The will was there, the means was there; all that lacked was conviction. I can only imagine where we would be today, had I followed my convictions and imagination to the fullest when the ideas first struck me. We would all be in a place that boggles the mind, and for this I am sorry.

Ken Whiting, my good friend, my peer, and my world champion has given me this opportunity to redeem myself. He approached me with the idea for this book, and asked me, as one of the leaders in the development of aerial moves to write that section. I hope that the basic explanation that I can give on the very foundations and basic concepts of aerial moves will enable readers to progress and learn the moves. Any failure to do so must ultimately fall upon my inability to correctly convey to you the most fundamental concepts of aerial moves.

I therefore preface this book with these words: there is nothing so important as an open mind. There is nothing so destructive to the learning curve as fear of failure, or vanity; the fear of appearing ridiculous as you try and fail, for fail you will, many times before you succeed. If it is of any consolation, it has taken me nearly a decade to learn and perfect all the skills that this book is attempting to teach you, and no one has fallen on his head more often than I.

You will need in many regards to unlearn all that you have previously learned. You will need to absorb these teachings, and inscribe them upon the palimpsest of your current skills.

Your free, open mind is your greatest asset.

ABOUT THE AUTHOR

During the summer of 1989, Ken picked up a kayak paddle for the first time. He was 14 years old at the time, and was taking a 5-day kayaking course on the Ottawa River. Little did Ken know that this week of paddling would set the course of his life. Four years later he postponed his plans for university and satisfied his need to play by travelling, paddling and working as a raft guide in Australia. Ken's addiction to whitewater only grew from this experience. In 1994, Ken's competitiveness broke through the surface as he began frequenting, and winning, freestyle competitions across the continent.

Three years later, in 1997, he reached his ultimate goal by winning the World Freestyle Kayaking Championships. Winning the World's was a major turning point in Ken's life as shortly afterwards he made the decision to develop a career within the whitewater industry that he loved so much. In 1998, Ken wrote and published 'The Playboater's Handbook', a reference for freestyle kayaking technique.

Following the great success of the book, Ken teamed up with Chris Emerick, a talented American videographer, and began producing instructional videos. Ken has now produced three best-selling and award-winning instructional kayaking videos, including 'Play Daze', 'SOAR', and 'Liquid Skills'. Ken's projects also provide him with a great means of exploring different parts of the world. He has paddled on over 200 rivers in 14 different countries including Japan, Honduras, Guatemala, Chile, Peru, New Zealand, Australia, as well as throughout Europe and North America.

Nowadays, Ken divides his time between the places that he has come to love the most. His winters are spent in Vancouver, BC and in Chile's Futaleufu Valley, while his summers are spent in the Ottawa Valley and on the road.

Ken has clearly become one of the most influential whitewater paddlers in the world. He continues to develop industry leading instructional tools and is a contributing editor to every North American paddlesports magazine, as well as to a number of international publications. Ken is also a partner in one of the world's premier kayak schools, Liquid Skills, and in the highly acclaimed adventure travel company, Kayak International. Through Kayak International and Liquid Skills, Ken teaches and leads trips around the world throughout the year. Though Ken spends less time competing on the pro circuit these days, he continues to be a leader of the freestyle kayaking movement as the volunteer Manager of the Canadian Freestyle Team, and as the freestyle representative within Whitewater Canada. For more info on Ken's activities, visit www.playboat.com.

Ken, Chris Emerick and Kevin Varette on the Futaleufu River, Chile.

CONTRIBUTORS

Thanks to all those who contributed their time and energy.

Corran Addison

South African born Corran Addison is undoubtedly one of the most recognized and respected whitewater personalities in the world. With 25 years of paddling experience, a deep passion for the sport, unquestionable natural talent, and an insatiable desire for advancement, Corran has played, and continues to play, a key role in the development of freestyle kayaking. To stay in touch with Corran's activities, check out www.2imagine.net

"Whether you like him or not, there is something you cannot take away from this paddling genius: his passion for boating. The legacy he gives to kayaking is not only huge, it is essential." - Kayak Session Magazine

Tyler Curtis

Tyler grew up on the banks of McKoy's Chute on the Ottawa River, what he considers to be the best rapid in the world. Though this undoubtedly helped push his kayaking career along, it is Tyler's passion for the sport, his competitive drive, and his raw talent that have allowed him to become a 3-time Canadian Freestyle Champion, and one of the top paddlers in the world. Aside from his full-time dedication towards pushing the sport to new levels, Tyler teaches kayaking clinics around the world and is an active contributor to magazines. For more information on Tyler and his current activities, visit www.riverplay.ca

Paul Villecourt

Paul Villecourt is a French photographer and whitewater paddler who is dedicated to capturing the sensations of adventure and outdoor sports. His passion for whitewater has taken him and his camera to all corners of the world, including New Zealand, Canada, US, Lebanon, Greece, Hawaii, and Chile. Paul is regarded as one of the finest whitewater photographers in the world and his work has been published in virtually every outdoor magazine in Europe and North America. For more info on Paul and his activities, visit www.villecourt.com.

Steve Fisher

Steve Fisher, a 25–year-old South African, has been competing and winning in the various disciplines of kayaking since the age of 13. This includes such events as grueling 100-mile down-river marathons, flatwater marathons, and slalom races. Over the past 5 years Steve has been focusing his attention on freestyle kayaking. Since that time he has clearly become one of the world's top kayakers actively pushing the sport to new levels with his aggressive, gung-ho attitude. As a result of Steve's relentless drive to succeed, he has made a career out of the sport he loves and is living the life he has always dreamed of. For more information about Steve and his latest activities, visit www.stevefisher.net

Tyler, Kevin and Ken, hanging out on the Futaleufu.

USING THIS BOOK

This book was written with the assumption that you are comfortable with the basics of whitewater kayaking and that you have an understanding of the different whitewater features that make up a rapid. Otherwise, this book was written for all levels of paddlers. It starts off by explaining how to choose the right equipment for your body type and paddling style. It then looks in detail at the fundamental concepts and skills that will be necessary for any play move. From there, the book dives into the specific playboating moves, starting with the most basic and working towards the most advanced. Whether you're an expert playboater or learning to surf your first wave, I urge you to read the 'Fundamental Concepts and Skills' sections of this book as it clarifies issues that will be referred to constantly.

Regardless of how dutifully you study this book and work on your technique, there are a few other ways that you can help your paddling progress. First of all, what we think we are doing is not always what we are doing. Take the time to video yourself trying the moves or the drill because you will likely pick out some things to work on. Secondly, be sure to watch the best paddlers in your area and take notice of how and where they are making the moves happen. Why re-invent the wheel? For this same reason, taking a playboating clinic can really help speed things along.

EQUIPMENT

"Big" EZ!?

Choosing the right kayak

If you're shopping for a new kayak, I have some good news and some bad news for you. The good news is that I guarantee there is a boat out there that will be perfect for your body type and paddling style. The bad news is that you can expect it to take some serious investigative work to find. In 2001 alone, there were over 20 new playboats introduced to the market! I'm going to do my best to make this sorting process as easy as possible for you.

Your body type is one of the biggest factors for picking a boat but you also need to make some personal decisions. You need to decide whether you can afford to get a kayak that will be used almost exclusively for play, or whether you are looking for more of an all-round playboat: i.e. something that you can confidently use for running rivers. You also need to consider whether you're going to be spending more time in shallow rivers, with small river features, or big rivers with big play features. Both of these decisions will greatly affect the type of boat you buy. Regardless, you'll want to choose a boat that meets your needs as you continue to improve. This means choosing a boat that is short (under 8'), has a planing hull, and is a reasonable width so that rolling and holding an edge are easy.

Exclusive Playboats vs All-Round Playboats

To make this as simple as possible, the smaller the playboat you choose, the more responsive it will be for aggressive freestyle moves. The larger the playboat you choose, the more forgiving and comfortable it will be, and the better it will be for other types of paddling. An unfortunate reality of freestyle kayaking is that unless you have very short legs, you can expect to be slightly uncomfortable in a playboat that is the ultimate size for you. The reason for this is that the less volume a boat has in the ends, the less air you'll need to force underwater for vertical moves, but the less space you'll have for your feet. A kayak with more volume in the ends will be more comfortable and more forgiving, but harder to throw around. Of course you can go too far in either direction, so spend some time finding a boat that provides a good balance of for you.

Volume of the Kayak

Your weight will have a major impact on the boat you choose. As a rule, a kayak becomes easier to throw around as it shrinks in volume, but it also becomes less forgiving. This means that smaller boats are edgier and will flush off waves and out of holes more easily, but they'll be a godsend when you're practicing moves on flatwater. Ideally, look for a boat that you can throw around on flatwater, but that provides enough volume to be slightly forgiving.

Big Water vs. Low Volume

Low volume rivers often have shallow pour-over holes, steep little waves, and small eddylines to play with. The shortest playboats work best in this situation. As rivers get larger in volume, the current moves faster, holes get bigger, and waves get faster. It is usually preferable to have a slightly longer boat for these rivers as they are faster, and you generally won't have to worry about hitting the bottom.

Boat Width

As a playboat gets wider, its planing surface grows. A large planing surface will let you flat spin very well and is generally more stable. On the downside, as a boat gets wider it also gets more difficult to move from edge to edge, and to roll. You can get away with using a wider boat by padding your seat so that you sit higher, but be sure not to raise your center of gravity too much or you're going to be flipping all the time. As a general rule, the taller and heavier you are, the wider the kayak you can get away with.

Boat Length

The effect of a playboat's length is simple. As a kayak gets shorter, it gets slower, but it becomes more manoeuvrable. The shortest boats are the best boats for low volume rivers and for aerial moves (loops, aerial blunts, space Godzilla's, etc…). Slightly longer boats provide more options on big volume rivers and are great for carving up waves and playing in bigger volume holes.

*An offset of 30 degrees
is a good choice*

Choosing your paddle

Choosing a paddle to suit your body size and paddling style is important. You'll need to consider the length of the paddle, the width of the paddle's shaft, and the size of the blades. Smaller paddlers should look for a paddle with slightly smaller blades and with a narrower shaft that makes gripping the paddle easiest. The stronger you are, the larger the paddle blades you'll be able to control. Using a paddle that's too long, or too large, will cost you some control and could put an undue amount of stress on your body. Next, you'll need to consider the offset of your paddle. The offset, or twist, refers to the difference in angles between the two blades. Traditional kayak paddles have blades that are offset at 90 degrees, but these days there's no reason to have a paddle with more than a 30 degree twist. This small amount of twist is easier on the wrists and comes in handy when both your blades are in the water at the same time. FYI: I'm around 6'3", 205 lbs, and I use a 204 cm paddle with big blades, and no twist at all.

Paddler Size	Big Blades	Small Blades
5' – 5'4"		188 - 194
5'4" – 5'8"	190 – 196	190 – 196
5'8" – 6'	194 - 198	194 - 198
6' – 6'4	198 - 204	

A general paddle size recommendation

More Playboating Gear

Dry Deck

One of the all-time best inventions for the playboater is the one-piece drytop and skirt, commonly referred to as the Dry Deck. The Dry Deck provides paddlers with total freedom around the waist as there is no skirt hugging the body and no drytop waistband to cinch up. Not only is this unbelievably comfortable but it allows paddlers to get the most out of their torso rotation as well.

Purifying Water Bottle

Playboaters are well known for being minimalists. If we don't absolutely need something, then we often won't bring it. I have to admit that this is somewhat understandable as extra weight does impact the performance of a playboat. It's ironic that although we spend the whole day on the water, we often end up dehydrated because we can carry only so much water with us (if we carry any at all). The Exstream purifying water bottle solves this problem as it allows you to carry an empty bottle that will provide safe drinking water at any time. This is one of the best inventions for playboaters and for any other outdoor enthusiast, as staying hydrated plays a major role in keeping energy levels up and letting you make the most of your day.

Paddle Wax/Tape

Playboating requires a combination of power and technique. Neither one on its own will do the trick. At times, you will need to pull or push on your paddle with every ounce of strength that you have so it is imperative that you have a good grip on your paddle. The best way to maintain a good grip on your paddle is with tape or with wax. One thing to consider is that you'll want to start with minimal grip on your paddle in order to build up some calluses. If you go with too much grip right away, you'll wear your hands raw after a full day of boating.

Playboating Life Jackets

With so much upper body and arm activity involved with whitewater paddling, life jackets can be one of the most inhibiting pieces of gear. For this reason, manufacturers have designed low-profile life jackets that minimize the interference with your movements without removing any of the actual flotation. They do this by moving the flotation away from the most active areas (shoulders, chest, sides, shoulder blades), and re-distribute it to the least active areas (stomach, mid-back). This greatly enhances a paddler's manoeuvrability. On the downside, these life jackets don't provide quite as much protection as others, and they aren't all designed for rescue situations. You'll want to have a second life jacket if you like to do different types of paddling.

Playboating Shoes

I'm sure you've heard it before, but you really should be paddling with some type of footwear. Not only does it make walking around on the rocks a whole lot safer, but it will cut down on the abuse your feet take when squeezed into a small boat. For a while, there weren't any viable options for footwear in playboats, as all water-shoes were bulky and stiff- great for walking around on the rocks, but impossible to fit in the tiny new boats. If they did fit inside, then they were worn out quickly because pressure points were not re-enforced. It didn't take water-shoe companies long to recognize this and to make the necessary changes. There is now a variety out there from which to choose. Some things to look for in a good playboating shoe include a thin, flexible sole, re-enforced big toe and heel, and minimal buckles/zippers.

The
Fundamental
Concepts

WARMING UP

Without a doubt your body is your most important tool. The stronger and more flexible you are, the better off you will be. This doesn't mean that whitewater kayaking needs to be a high impact sport. It is amazing how far good technique will get you. In the same breath, power is essential for getting the most out of your kayak because even with perfect technique, sometimes you'll just need to push or pull harder!

It should go without saying that a warm-up routine, followed by stretching, is an invaluable way to keep the body healthy, but most paddlers totally ignore their lower bodies. The lower body is actually very important to warm up for a day on the water. In particular, tight hips will impede your boat tilts and cause lower back pain, and tight hamstrings can dramatically affect your ability to lean forward. Keeping your entire body strong and limber will definitely help improve your paddling, but it will also make sitting in a small kayak a lot more comfortable.

THE POWER POSITION AND SHOULDER SAFETY

Shoulder safety should be a real concern for all paddlers and there are two simple rules that, when followed, will go a long way towards keeping your arms protected. 1. Don't overextend your arms. 2. Maintain a power position with your arms.

1. The idea of not overextending your arms is a simple concept to appreciate, but it isn't always so simple to apply. When you're getting tossed around in whitewater, the desire to keep your head above the water can easily over-ride any safe paddling practices. Try staying as relaxed as possible, and fight the urge to use massive 'Geronimo' braces.

2. You may be asking yourself what the 'power position' is. It's actually quite simple. When looking at your body from above, let's consider an invisible line that passes through both shoulders. We'll refer to this as the 'shoulder line'. Now consider another line that divides your body into two equal halves. We'll call this the 'mid line'. The power position simply involves keeping your hands in front of your shoulder line and preventing your hands from crossing your mid line. In so doing, you will maintain a rectangle with your arms, paddle and chest. With this rectangle formed, you get the most power from your paddle and your shoulders stay in the safest position. When your hands move behind your shoulder line your arm is in a very vulnerable position. Does this mean that you can't safely reach to the back of your kayak? Not at all! But what it does mean is that in order to reach to the back of your kayak you'll need to rotate your whole torso so that you can keep your hands in the power position. You now have one more reason to separate your upper and lower body movements and use the power of torso rotation!

1. Poor torso rotation: the rear hand falls behind the shoulder line and the front hand crosses the mid-line.

2. The Power Position: the whole upper body turns so that both hands stay in front of the shoulder line, neither cross the mid-line, and the arms, paddle and chest form a rectangle.

CARVING AND SKIDDING

Playboats are designed to turn very effectively in two different ways. Their wide, flat hulls allow them to skid, while the sharp edges allow them to carve. Both of these features come in really handy in different situations. Take front surfing for example. When you want to carve back and forth, you'll use the sharp edges of your boat. When you want to do a flat spin, you'll keep your boat as flat as possible.

Just as with downhill skiing or snowboarding, the key to carving is getting on edge and preventing your tail end from sliding out. Most paddlers have a tougher time carving than spinning out because it requires balancing on edge, so we're going to look at edging in more detail. We'll then look at some drills that will improve your edging and balance.

Holding the boat on edge lets you carve

Keeping the boat flat lets you skid

EDGING

Every paddler needs to be able to quickly and comfortably get his or her boat on edge, then hold it there. To hold a boat steadily on edge you'll need to develop your balance on a single hip. Like any other skill, this will take practice. Ultimately, you should be able to hold your boat on a very steep edge with minimal wobble.

Start by shifting your weight from both butt cheeks onto a single butt cheek/hip. Staying balanced like this will require you to keep your upper body and head over the kayak. You should feel your stomach and side muscles working to keep your body positioned like this. Your knees are now responsible for modifying and steadying your boat tilt. By pulling up on the top knee and pushing down with the other knee, you can tilt your boat more aggressively, though this will make balancing more difficult.

A great way to practice holding different boat tilts is to paddle in a straight line with your boat on edge. You should be able to maintain a steady forward or backward stroke while holding your boat on almost any tilt. When you have developed the freedom to take strokes while balancing your kayak on edge, you have taken a major step towards being able to perform any play move.

Edging involves shifting your weight onto a single butt cheek/hip.

Developing the balance to hold your boat on edge while leaving your paddle free to take strokes is a major step towards advanced paddling techniques.

Body Position

When I talk about body positions, I'll be referring to the different forward and backward leans that you'll use. For any other 'body position' the only thing that is important is that your head and weight stay over the kayak. If your weight falls off to the side, you're going to flip.

There are three body positions that will be referred to throughout this book: an aggressive position, a neutral position, and a defensive position. An aggressive position refers to leaning forward. A defensive position means leaning back. A neutral position means sitting up straight. We call leaning forward 'aggressive' as it usually indicates that the paddler is taking control of the situation. We call leaning back 'defensive' as it is the natural reaction when we find ourselves in an uncomfortable situation. In this defensive position, we find ourselves reacting to the things that happen rather than taking charge. It is important to understand that any forward or backward lean should stem from the hips. The position that you'll use is dependent on your situation, but in general, the ideal paddling position is sitting up straight, with a slight lean forward in what we call a 'moderately

This moderately aggressive position is your 'default' body position

POWER VS TECHNIQUE

aggressive position'. This tends to be the best paddling position because the majority of flips result from the stern edges of the kayak being caught. This aggressive position helps to keep the stern edges out of the water. It will also provide you with the most control over your boat edging and will let you take the most powerful strokes. Keep in mind that maintaining this moderately aggressive position is simply a guideline. If you need to lean aggressively backward or forward, don't hesitate to do so. Just remember to get your body back into this moderately aggressive position as soon as you can.

From the very beginning I was taught that kayaking is all about technique. I was told that if I used the right technique while working co-operatively with the power of the river, I would be able to perform any move that I wanted. There is no doubt that good technique is crucial for any paddler to develop, but when it comes to performing many of the latest play moves, technique alone won't do the trick. There comes a point when you simply need to pull harder! Does this limit who can perform some of the moves? Yes, it does to some degree. Luckily though, manufacturers have recognized this and are continually developing kayaks that make the moves easier for paddlers of all shapes and sizes.

When you watch a great paddler on the water, the moves usually look smooth and sometimes even effortless. How can it be so easy? Well believe it or not, the moves usually aren't effortless! The pros are working hard to make them happen! What separates these great paddlers from other paddlers is their ability to apply all of their power to a move, without sacrificing technique. This is why it tends to look so smooth. It is for this same reason that Tiger Woods can swing his hardest and still drive a ball incredibly straight, while the rest of us (Kevin in particular) watch our balls slice madly when swinging at full speed. What this means is that you need to start by learning the correct technique. Once you've got it, then you can start applying more and more power. If things start going astray, then slow down and re-establish your good technique. Ultimately, your goal is to put everything you have into a move while maintaining perfect technique.

The
Fundamental
Skills

THE 3 GOLDEN RULES OF PADDLING

The 3 Golden Rules of whitewater paddling are essential concepts that all playboaters need to understand and apply. You need to separate your body movements, maintain control of your kayak with an active blade, and use the power of your torso. We'll start by looking at what these rules mean and why they're so important. You should then recognize these concepts as they are applied throughout the book.

#1   Separate your body movements

Good playboaters have learned to let their upper and lower bodies work independently, yet co-operatively with each other. This means there needs to be a distinct separation of movements at the hips. Most obviously this applies to the forward and backward leans that you'll use, but even more importantly, this is what makes it possible to balance a kayak on edge and to incorporate torso rotation into your moves.

#2   Maintain control with an active blade

The short boats of today are incredibly responsive. This makes them very easy to turn, but it's also easy to lose control of them as even the smallest river features will push them around. The only way to maintain control of your kayak is to have an active blade in the water. This means it's important to get your next stroke in the water as soon as one stroke is finished. By having an active blade in the water, you can take an active role in deciding where you'll go, rather than always reacting to the things that happen to your kayak.

Staying loose at the hips/waist allows you to edge your boat and rotate your torso for added power.

#3   Use the power of your torso

All paddle strokes should use much more than just arm and shoulder muscles. You need to use the power of your whole upper body for any stroke that you take. Torso rotation is the way to incorporate your front and side stomach muscles into your strokes. Using these larger muscles will let you harness the most power and will improve your stamina as your efforts are spread over more muscles. Torso rotation is also an important concept for keeping your shoulders safe, as we discussed in the 'Shoulder Safety' segment.

There are three components to torso rotation: the winding up of the body, the planting of a pivot blade, and the unwinding of the body. Winding up the body means turning your upper body at the waist so your chest no longer faces the direction that your kayak does. Once your body is wound up, your paddle gets planted in the water as a pivot. As you push or pull on this pivot blade, your knees and stomach muscles together will pull your body back to its position of rest. The act of using stomach muscles, along with your knees, to return your body to its position of rest is referred to as unwinding the body. Think of your body as an elastic band. The more you wind it up, the more power you'll have available to you. Though there's no need to fully wind up your body for every stroke, your stomach muscles should be involved with each and every stroke you take.

Your paddle is your steering wheel, so keep it in the water whenever possible.

The body is wound up and the paddle is planted firmly in the water.

As the paddle pushes away from the kayak, the stomach and knees help pull the kayak around, unwinding the body.

Note how the upper body moves from leaning back to leaning forward during the back sweep. This body movement gives the back sweep more power and more leverage.

Brace Yourself

Bracing refers to the action of using your paddle blade to stop yourself from flipping over. Though bracing is most commonly used for recovery after being knocked off balance, it should also be used as a preventative measure. With experience you'll be able to anticipate the water knocking you in a certain direction. With this foresight, you'll actually brace to prevent yourself from being knocked off balance. Eventually, you should be using more of these preventative braces than recovery braces.

There are two types of braces that you'll find useful: the low brace and the high brace. It's important to understand that the main function of these braces is not to push boat and body back to the upright position, but rather to stop your flipping momentum and to provide a platform that will allow your hips and knees to do the rest (just like a roll). With regard to which brace you should use, it's totally dependent on your situation. In general, the low brace works best for quick recoveries, while the high brace is considerably more powerful and tends to get used when you get thrown further over on your side. As long as you don't overextend your arms for either brace, then both can be used safely and effectively.

Keeping your arms close to the body is always a good idea.

The Low Brace

The low brace involves curling your wrists forward so that the non-power faces of your paddle blades are facing the water. It is this non-power face that will be providing the bracing power. Now bring your upper elbow in close against your side and reach out with the blade that will be bracing at 90-degrees to the direction of your kayak. The further out you reach, the more leverage you'll get from your brace, but be careful not to overextend your arms as this will put your shoulder in a vulnerable position. Your arms are in a relatively safe position as long as your upper arm doesn't cross your chest and your hands stay in the power position at all times (in front of your shoulder line). From this position you can smack the water, which should provide the momentary support needed for your hips and knees to snap the boat upright and to get your weight back over your kayak. To get more support from your brace than the initial slap can provide, sweep your paddle forward to your toes with a sculling angle that allows you to keep constant pressure on the back of the paddle.

The High Brace

The high brace involves cocking your wrists back so that the power faces of your paddle blades are at the ready. Again, your upper elbow gets tucked into your side while you reach out at 90-degrees to your kayak. The further you reach to the side, the more leverage you will get from your brace. With that said, you have to be careful not to overextend your arm and put your shoulder at risk. To ensure you aren't putting your shoulders in a dangerous position, your upper arm stays tucked into your side and doesn't reach across your chest. It's also very important that your hands stay low in front of your body, never reaching above eye level. From this position you can slap the water and get the momentary support needed to right the kayak with your hips and knees.

Because this brace often gets used when an aggressive recovery is needed, it is common for the paddle to end up fairly deep in the water. To recover from this and to get more support from your high brace, you'll need to keep your paddle active with a sculling motion. The most effective sculling combination is a quick sweep to the stern, followed by a full sweep to the bow with the wrists cocked back so that the power face continues to work all the way to your toes.

THROW IT INTO REVERSE

Most paddlers have developed a confident and powerful forward stroke, but few can boast the same for their backstroke. Considering that virtually all advanced playboating moves involve spinning around and spending half the time facing downstream, doesn't it make sense that your backstroke be as efficient as your forward stroke? If you haven't tried back paddling lately, then next time you're on the water, give 50 backstrokes a whirl. I think you'll find your stroke could use some practice and furthermore, you'll probably discover that your shoulders tire extremely quickly. Your shoulders tire so quickly because you're using a different set of muscles from those used for the forward stroke. The fronts of your shoulders are now getting a workout. This is an important weakness to isolate

The backstroke is the most common initiation stroke, so it's well worth taking the time to make it as strong as possible.

for a number of reasons. First of all, the backstroke is the most common initiating stroke, used for cartwheels, blunts, kick-flips and all sorts of other moves. Secondly, the most common whitewater kayaking injury is the shoulder dislocation. For anatomical reasons, the shoulder displaces forward over 90% of the time and having weak shoulder muscles is certainly not helping to prevent this from happening. Though strengthening the fronts of your shoulders won't stop a dislocation from taking place, it could make the small difference that extends your paddling life.

With all this said, it should make sense that your warm-up includes at least 50 backstrokes, with a focus on using the proper technique. Here are some things to consider when practicing your backstroke. Since playboats are so edgy, it's more important than ever to back paddle with an aggressive body position. This forward leaning position gives you the most control over your kayak, but more importantly, it helps keep your stern edges from catching water. Sometimes though, paddling in an aggressive position isn't enough to keep your stern edges from diving underwater, especially when you're paddling against current, crossing an eddyline, or otherwise accelerating. There is another technique you can use. By tilting your boat slightly and very briefly into each stroke you can slice your bow underwater, which keeps your stern on top of the water. How much you actually pull your bow underwater will depend on the particular situation, but remember that your backstroke is most efficient when your boat is flat, so be careful not to overuse this boat tilt technique. As for the backstroke itself, the stroke begins just behind your hip and ends at your toes. At first you'll find yourself doing lots of back sweep strokes to correct your angle, but as you get more comfortable going backward think about keeping your top hand around shoulder level to get the most push from your stroke. Another way to make the stroke more effective is to use the power of your whole upper body. Turning your chest to face your knee when you plant each stroke will help wind your body up. As you unwind your body, you'll get your large torso muscles working for you.

When you're comfortable with your backstroke, start fooling around with backward eddy turns and ferries. The more awareness you build with your back to the main current, the sooner you'll nail the most advanced moves.

Practice backward eddy turns. When crossing the eddline maintain an aggressive body position, keep your top hand at shoulder level and tilt your boat into your stroke.

THE PIVOT TURN

The pivot turn is the most powerful and effective means of turning your kayak and it is also a crucial skill for all advanced playboating moves. It is such an important skill because the pivot turn requires a combination of fine edge control, balance, and power. It also relies on your understanding of how to maintain spin momentum. This is a move that you NEED to practice! Because of its importance, we're going to look at the pivot turn from the very beginning.

The pivot turn is basically an ultra-powerful and effective sweep stroke during which one end of your kayak is pulled underwater, bringing the other end into the air. We're going to start by making sure that everyone is using the same sweep stroke technique. This may sound very basic, but the sweep stroke has been taught in a variety of different ways over the years. There are good reasons for using the different techniques, but with playboats, there is only one technique that you should ever use.

Starting from the top, you should turn your kayak in the same way you would turn your car. This means looking in the direction you wish to go, rather than directly in front of yourself! With the sweep stroke, you do this by turning to face the direction in which you intend to turn. By turning your whole upper body so that your head and chest

Keep your eyes on where you're going throughout the sweep stroke.

face in this direction, you also effectively wind up the body.

With your body wound up, plant your sweep securely in the water at your toes. When pulling on the sweep stroke, your top hand should stay between chest and chin height and your paddle should sweep as far out to the side of the kayak as possible. Meanwhile, your knees and stomach muscles can pull your legs around, effectively unwinding your body.

The same ideas apply to the back sweep. Turn your head and body in the direction that you will be pulling your bow, plant your stroke deeply, then pull your legs around as you push away with your back sweep. For starters, practice both these sweep strokes while keeping your boat flat to the water.

The head and body lead the way through the back sweep, a key initiating stroke for many play moves

Stern Pivot Turn

Once you're comfortable with the concept of looking ahead, you're ready to turn your sweep stroke into a powerful pivot turn. We'll start by looking at the 'stern pivot turn' which involves slicing the stern of your kayak underwater. By sinking your stern, your bow will lift off the water and you'll spin around incredibly quickly and easily. The stern pivot turn can be initiated with either a back sweep or a front sweep, but we'll look at using the front sweep as it is a more powerful stroke. To sink your stern you'll need to do a couple of things as you take your sweep stroke: tilt your kayak towards your stroke and throw

To initiate the stern pivot turn, tilt your kayak towards your front sweep and throw your weight back momentarily (getting forward again as soon as you can). Note how aggressively the head leads the way.

To avoid 'hitting the wall' you must level off your boat tilt before your stroke has finished. Here, the stroke finishes, and the boat is already level. The kayak will now continue on course.

your weight back momentarily (getting forward again as soon as you can). Your sweep stroke should now be pulling down on the water, as well as out to the side, to help pull your bow into the air. Now that your stern is slicing underwater and your sweep stroke is reaching its end, you need to take quick action in order to maintain the spin momentum you've built up.

Maintaining spin momentum comes down to a very simple rule: after pulling an end of your kayak underwater, you must level off your boat tilt BEFORE your initiating stroke has finished. If you don't level off your tilt quickly enough, you'll 'hit the wall'. 'Hitting the wall' means that all the spin momentum you've worked hard to build will be instantly lost as the buoyancy of the end you've pulled underwater takes that end back to the surface in the same direction from which it came. If you do level off your tilt in time, then the buoyancy energy of the end that is underwater will keep your spin going as that end corkscrews its way back to the surface. To level off your boat tilt, think about pulling upward with the knee that is on the sweeping side of your kayak. You should also think about this in terms of a weight transition. When your kayak is on edge, your weight is balanced on a single hip/butt cheek. When your boat is levelled off, your weight is balanced squarely on both butt cheeks. You need to make this weight transition before your stroke has finished.

Bow Pivot Turn

You can also perform bow pivot turns, though they are a bit trickier to do. In this case you are attempting to force the bow of your kayak underwater, which is most easily done with a back sweep. To submerge your bow you'll need to do a couple of things as you take your back sweep: tilt your kayak into the back sweep and throw your weight aggressively forward. Once your bow is underwater, the key remains in levelling off your boat tilt before you hit the wall. Because your back sweep isn't as powerful as your forward sweep, and because the bow of your kayak has more volume than your stern, you can't expect to force your bow down as effectively as you can pull your stern underwater. This means that you're going to need to level off your boat tilt more quickly in order to avoid hitting the wall by pushing your weight onto both butt cheeks.

When you think you've got the pivot turns nailed, start applying more power and force your ends underwater even more aggressively. Having the fine edge control and balance to consistently nail these pivot turns will take lots of practice, but will go a very long way towards helping your overall playboating. So keep working on it!

The key to the bow pivot turn is tilting your boat into your back sweep and throwing your weight forward as you take the stroke. Before the back sweep finishes, you need to push your weight onto both butt cheeks to level off your boat tilt. The bow pivot turn isn't as powerful as the stern pivot turn, so prepare to level off your boat tilt as soon as you begin slicing the bow underwater.

THE POWER STROKE

The power stroke is a vertical forward stroke that is designed to help your playboat carve, unlike most other strokes that help your kayak spin. This stroke can give a playboater a major forward boost when it's needed, such as when you are setting up and trying to build speed for advanced moves like the blunt, or when you're crossing powerful eddylines. It's also a great way to develop the balance and edge control that are essential for any play move. We're going to look at the power stroke while at the same time developing an exercise that will let you practice it, and improve your balance.

The goal of the exercise is to carve a full circle using only power strokes. Starting with some forward speed, get your kayak carving by taking a small sweep stroke and tilting your boat on edge. From this point on, you'll use only vertical forward strokes (power strokes) on the inside of your turn to keep your boat carving in a circle. Your success in continuing to carve a circle is based on two things: your ability to balance your kayak steadily on edge, and your ability to take forward strokes with your paddle kept vertical. These vertical forward strokes focus your power on moving the boat directly forward. If your stroke isn't quite vertical, then it will effectively be working against the carving momentum of your kayak. Ultimately, this will break the circle that you are trying to carve, as your boat will start turning in the other direction.

Carving a continuous circle using only strokes on the inside of the turn.

Commit to getting your paddle vertical by reaching across your boat with the top hand.

The key to making your forward strokes vertical is reaching across your kayak with your top hand, while keeping your bottom hand in close to the kayak. This is a very committing thing to do, as your paddle cannot act as any type of a brace in this position. You are relying almost 100% on balance. Because of this, it is only natural to move your bottom hand out to the side, where it can provide a small brace. The problem with this is that your paddle won't be vertical and your forward stroke will again be fighting your carving momentum. Commit! Expect to flip while trying this! It will take plenty of practice, but soon you'll be able to balance your boat on a steady edge without the support of your paddle. Then, with continuous vertical power strokes, you should be able to keep carving indefinitely.

As we discussed in the 'Power vs Technique' chapter, you have two goals when working on this exercise. Your first goal is to develop the balance and technique to take these vertical power strokes and keep your boat carving. Once you can do this comfortably, start adding power to the equation. Ultimately, you should be able to keep carving these circles as you put 100% power into your strokes. One of the ways to maximize your power strokes is by thrusting your hips forward with each stroke. Think as much about thrusting your hips past your paddle as pulling your paddle alongside the boat. As your balance improves, you'll even find that you can reach your top hand so far across your kayak that your strokes are actually even past vertical. This will guarantee that you aren't fighting your carving momentum and is a great demonstration of balance and commitment.

Whitewater

The Playboater's Perspective

As the sport of freestyle kayaking has evolved, so has the way that paddlers look at a river. The bottom line is that the river has become a bigger and better playground! Eddies used to be safe havens where paddlers could relax before making the next move downstream. For the playboater, an eddy is a place where one can leisurely scope out the best wave, or it's the best place from which to catch a wave. Eddylines used to be the 'hurdles' of the river, but now they're great squirt spots and, at their origin, there is often a corner in which to throw cartwheels.

The biggest changes have come from the way we look at waves. Playboaters are looking to surf a much wider range of waves, whether small, large, steep, breaking, etc… What about those big, beautiful, glassy, Dancer-style waves that our short boats aren't fast enough to catch? Are they going to waste? No way! These are perfect launching pads for wave wheels and kick flips! The same changes in perception can be seen when we look at holes. We used to look at a hole and say 'I don't know about that one! It's got a pretty big recirc!' We now look at that same hole and say 'It's powerful enough to stick a Tricky Whu! Wonder if it's deep enough?'

Regardless of these changes, the ability to read whitewater remains an important skill to develop. Like any other skill, it will require lots of practice. Though endless sessions at your local playspot will take your paddling a long way, to really work on your river reading skills you'll need some variety. The greater the diversity of waves and holes you surf, the more experience you'll have to draw upon. You can always tell experienced playboaters by their swiftness in identifying the sweet spots on a new play feature. It's almost instantaneous, while less experienced paddlers will take much longer.

In this chapter, we're going to take a quick look at some common river features so everyone is on the same wavelength regarding terminology.

Holes

Holes come in an endless number of shapes and sizes, and while a great playhole can bring paddlers from all over the world, a nasty hole can repel paddlers like the plague. Being able to differentiate between a friendly hole and a nasty hole isn't overly difficult, but it will take experience. While building this experience, be sure to use your common sense. If you don't see paddlers playing in a hole, then there's probably a reason why. If you're not sure if a hole will be fun to surf or not, leave it alone. There really is nothing more frightening and confidence crushing than getting thrashed by a hole.

When deciding whether or not a hole is friendly, you must consider three things. Is it an easy hole to balance in? Is it an easy hole to get out of? Is it a safe hole?

Holes can be placed in one of three categories. There are wave-holes, true holes and pour-overs. Wave-holes are also referred to as breaking waves and they represent the friendliest form of a hole. These holes are formed when a standing wave is too steep to hold its form, so the peak of the wave is consistently breaking. These holes are the easiest to surf and to move around in, as the greenwater flows in at a very low angle, so paddlers don't need to tilt their boats much to stay balanced. True holes are holes formed when water pours over a rock or a shelf, creating a hole with its seam in the trough. These holes tend to be more powerful than breaking waves and are often more difficult to get out of because the greenwater flows into the hole on a steeper angle, forcing paddlers to hold a more aggressive boat tilt to stay balanced. On the upside, true holes can offer the most variety for vertical moves. Pour-overs are the most difficult holes to surf, as they are formed when water pours very steeply over an object. Due to the steep angle of the greenwater flowing into the hole, paddlers must hold a very aggressive boat tilt. This makes it incredibly difficult to stay balanced over the kayak and makes it difficult to get out as well. These holes also tend to be the most dangerous as

— Corner
— Boil line
— Foam pile
— Greenwater
— Seam
— Trough

the object creating the pour-over is often close to the surface and very little water is allowed to pass downstream.

Clearly, the steepness of the greenwater flowing into the hole plays a major role in deciding whether or not a hole is friendly, but there are a couple of other things to consider. First of all, some holes can be easier to get out of than others based on the position of the corners. If the corners are further downstream than the hole's trough, then the river will naturally push you towards them, helping you exit. If the corners of a hole are even with, or further upstream than the trough of the hole, then the hole will be more difficult to get out of, as you'll be fighting the river to reach the exit points.

Waves

Waves are generally a lot less complicated than holes, though they obviously still come in all shapes and sizes. They are generally formed in one of two ways: by water flowing over an obstacle and piling up on itself below, or by moving water being constricted and forced to pile up on itself. Either way, waves are the most user-friendly features on the river, as they involve the least amount of conflicting currents. Even if a wave is breaking, the vast majority of the water is flowing downstream and is relatively predictable, unlike holes and eddies, which have large amounts of water moving in opposite directions.

Unlike holes, it is difficult to differentiate in detail between advantageous and detrimental features of a wave, aside from the most obvious concerns such as the depth of the water. Different waves are good for different moves. In general, the steeper a wave is, the more potential it will have for different moves. The same can be said for the shoulders of the wave. The better the shoulders of a wave are, the more potential there is to perform a variety of moves.

Peak
Spin corner

Shoulder

Greenwater

Wave / Breaking Wave

Eddies

As I mentioned earlier in this book, catching a wave can often be the toughest part of front or back surfing. A big reason for this is the lack of understanding of the dynamics of eddies. When moving from eddy to wave, one must decide upon a plan of action. If this plan gets altered as early as when you're leaving the eddy, then the chances of catching a wave will drop dramatically. The most important eddy characteristic to understand is the difference in eddy currents. An eddy is not simply a uniform area of slack water. There are currents of different speeds in an eddy that must be considered. Luckily, we can predict where the different currents will be found and can modify our plan of action to take this into account. In general, the further away from the eddyline you get, the faster the current will be. This is obviously important to note, as timid paddlers will naturally want to be as far as possible from the main current or eddyline. By moving further away, paddlers will actually be putting themselves in faster current and can easily get pushed right back into the main current. This faster current also has a tendency of messing around with a

paddler's plan of action when trying to catch a wave. With that said, you're generally better off hanging out very close to the eddyline whether you're relaxing or setting yourself up to exit an eddy, as this is where the slackest water can be found.

River Right vs Surfer's Right

In the past, when giving directions on a river, one would always

use the river right and river left terminology. This made perfect sense when a paddler's main goal was to get from point A to B, and everything was looked at in terms of moving downstream. Now that paddlers spend so much time surfing and facing upstream, we need to adopt a less confusing system of communicating directions. This is where surfer's right and left come in, and has long been used by the ocean surfing crowd. The surfer's right and surfer's left terms refer to directions from the perspective of someone front surfing a wave. This actually completely reverses the directions. River right is actually going to be the surfer's left.

The idea of introducing the surfer's directions isn't to replace the standard communication system, but to provide a cleaner means of describing things from a surfer's perspective. Both systems make great sense in different circumstances and should continue to get used.

The crowd is on the river right, but the surfer's left.

The Clock

Throughout this book, we'll be using time to describe the direction that your kayak points. 12 o'clock will be considered pointing directly upstream, and 6 o'clock will be considered pointing directly downstream. Similarly, pointing perpendicular to the main current to the surfer's left will be considered 9 o'clock, and to the surfer's right will be 3 o'clock.

12 o'clock

3 o'clock

6 o'clock

Flatwater and Eddline Moves

STERN SQUIRTS

The stern squirt involves slicing the stern of your kayak underwater and pivoting around with your bow in the air: basically a stern pivot turn initiated with a back sweep. It is often done when crossing an eddyline where the main current can help pull your stern underwater, but you can also squirt on flatwater. Stern squirting is a great way of practicing many of the skills that are essential for advanced moves and you'll become more comfortable with being on end. Keep in mind that playboats are designed to get vertical easily, so getting vertical on a powerful eddyline doesn't necessarily mean that you're using proper technique. In order to focus on using the proper technique, practice your stern squirts on flatwater, or on weak eddylines that make it more challenging to get vertical.

Wherever you practice the squirt, your ultimate goal should be a full 360-degree turn from the initial stroke. Contrary to popular belief, the ideal squirt is not a vertical move! Your bow should be lifted anywhere from 30 to 80 degrees. By keeping it under vertical you can stay balanced while pivoting around on your stern. The size of your kayak relative to your body weight will certainly have a bearing on how vertical you can get, so everyone can't expect to be able to lift the bow high into the air. Let's start by looking at the stern squirt on flatwater.

The key to stern squirting is keeping your weight over your kayak at all times. This is going to require a real separation of your upper and lower bodies. Start with some forward speed and then establish spin momentum with a light sweep stroke, while keeping your boat flat so that your stern slides out instead of carving. Once you've slid out to 90 degrees, it's time to initiate the squirt. Your head and body must always lead the way, which means they turn aggressively to the inside of the spin. This will effectively wind up your body. As you wind up, lean back and reach to plant a powerful back sweep behind your stern. Both your hands should be over the side of the kayak and your back arm should be straight. You also need to tilt your kayak to the outside of the turn so that your back sweep pushes your stern underwater. With your body wound up and your boat on edge, engage your back sweep. Plant your blade deeply underwater so your back sweep can push upwards while at the same time pushing away from the kayak. Pushing upwards with your paddle helps to force your stern underwater. As you push on your paddle, you now have the support needed for your stomach muscles to pull the bow

of the kayak up and around. You are now effectively unwinding your body. Your back sweep should be reaching its end once you've turned 180 degrees from your initial position. At this point, your stern should be underwater and your body should have returned to an upright sitting position. This upright position is much more stable and is absolutely essential for the more advanced moves. Now, the success of your stern squirt relies on your ability to avoid 'hitting the wall'. From the Pivot Turn segment, you'll remember that this means leveling off the tilt on your kayak before your stroke has finished. By leveling off your tilt, you'll maintain your spin momentum and your kayak will continue to spin around as the stern fights its way to the surface. This is the only way you'll be able to perform a full 360 spin from your initiating back sweep.

Once your kayak has slid out to 90 degrees, you'll initiate the squirt with your head and body aggressively leading the way, your boat tilted to the outside of the turn, and a back sweep planted as far back as possible.

If planted deeply enough, you can help pull your bow into the air by pushing up as well as out to the side with your back sweep. Before this stroke has finished, make sure you have shifted your weight onto both butt cheeks and leveled off your boat tilt

With boat tilt leveled off, your spin momentum will continue to take you around while you guide your bow back to the water's surface, completing a full 360 with a single back sweep.

To make the most out of your stern squirt practice, start with a relatively small boat tilt, which you can then increase as your balance and power improves. Ultimately, you'll be able to initiate your squirt with your boat tilted at around a 30-degree angle. You should also focus on these three elements: winding up and unwinding your body using your stomach muscles, finishing your back sweep with your body in an upright position, and leveling the tilt on your kayak before the back sweep is finished. Once you can routinely put these elements together, not only will you have a great stern squirt, but you'll have opened the doors to virtually every other advanced playboating move.

Overview – Stern Squirt

- Establish forward speed and let your kayak spin out to 90 degrees.
- With your boat tilted to the outside of the turn, wind your body up, and plant a back sweep as deeply and as far back as possible.
- Pull up and away with your back sweep as you slice your stern underwater and pull your bow around with your stomach and knees.
- Finish your back sweep with your body sitting upright, and your boat tilt leveled.
- With your spin momentum continuing to take you around, you should be able to do a full 360 from the initiation stroke.

STERN PIROUETTES

Once you've got the power, balance and edge control to complete a full 360 stern squirt from a single stroke, it's time to look at how to keep your squirt going. This is what the stern pirouette is: a continued stern squirt using a bow draw technique.

As soon as your initial back sweep has finished, lead aggressively with your head and upper body and plant your paddle right out to the side of your hip with an open power face (wrists cocked back so that the power face is facing forward). With the whole blade submerged, pull it forward to your knee. When the stroke is finished, close the power face (curl your wrists forward), slice that same blade back out to the side of your hip, and do it all again. Throughout this series of bow draws, your head and body must continue to aggressively lead the way. Not only does this provide power for the move by winding your body up, but it also helps to protect your shoulders from ending up in a vulnerable position. For the same reason you also want to make sure that you keep your top hand in front of your body at all times and don't let it get too high.

With head and body leading the way, the bow draw starts out to the side of the body, with the wrists cocked back to open the power face of the paddle.

Once the bow draw has been pulled all the way in, the boat needs to be levelled off to avoid hitting the wall. Note how aggressively the head leads the way.

With wrists curled forward, slice the paddle back out to the side of the kayak, open it up, and then draw it to the knee once again.

Keep in mind everything we talked about in the 'Pivot Turn' segment of this book, because this move is basically a continuous pivot turn. If you don't have an active blade pulling your stern around, then your boat needs to be level. If not, you'll hit the wall and kill your pirouette. This means that when you are actively pulling on the draw, you can edge your boat and force your stern further underwater. But, when your draw has reached your knee, you must level off any boat tilt before slicing that blade back out for the next draw. Having the balance, power, and the edge control to keep a stern pirouette going is a major achievement. At this point you have the tools necessary for any of the advanced moves.

Overview – Stern Pirouettes

- Use an open-face bow draw to pull your bow around.
- When the draw reaches your knee, close the power face, and slice the draw back to where it began.
- Lead aggressively and continuously with the head and body

Advanced Tip: For those who have become proficient at stern pirouettes, here's something new to try. Instead of simply slicing your paddle back to its starting position after each draw, there is a way of applying non-stop pressure with your paddle, which allows you to continuously force your stern underwater. This involves moving your paddle in a teardrop pattern, rather than the linear pattern we have been considering. You'll start the same way, but as your draw approaches your knee, keep the power face open and start pulling towards your body. The draw should end up closer to your hip this time. Without pause, keep a semi-open power face and start pushing out and behind your hip using the back of the blade. This 'back-stroke' allows you to you're your boat on edge and continue to work your stern underwater. Once you reach your starting point out to the side of your hip, you're back to square one and ready to bow draw to your knee again.

SCREW-UPS

The screw-up is a recovery technique that evolved from over-vertical stern squirts. It is now one of the best recovery techniques for playboaters because it can be used virtually anytime your bow passes vertical, whether you're screwing around on the flatwater or in a hole. The idea behind the screw-up is quite simple. It is a means of avoiding the misfortune of landing on your head when a move passes vertical. You do this by making a very early commitment to a roll.

The best way to practice the screw-up is to intentionally go past vertical while stern squirting on an eddyline, so this is where we're going to start. Eventually the motions will become natural for you and you'll instinctively use this recovery in many different situations.

So you've crossed through the eddyline and have initiated an aggressive stern squirt with a powerful back sweep. As soon as it's clear that you're going past vertical, it's time to initiate the screw-up. The direction of your squirt will dictate which side you will screw-up/roll on. One direction will let you use the squirt's spin momentum to your advantage, while the other will be fighting this spin momentum. As a rule, you'll want to screw-up/roll in the same direction that you're turning. This means that if you initiated the squirt with a back sweep on the left (which would be pulling the bow to the left), you'll want to screw-up using that same left blade to roll. The key to making the screw-up happen is leading the move with your head and body and throwing your weight back so that you can grab water with your paddle as far from your hip and as quickly as possible.

With a stern squirt initiated on the left side, you'll be using this same left blade for the screw-up.

As the boat passes vertical, turn and lead the move with your head and body. Grab water with your paddle as far from your hip and as quickly as possible.

The body swings forward as the kayak is rotated under the body with the hips.

The paddle provides the purchase for the move, so the quicker you grab water, the quicker you can begin recovering from the over-vertical position. Once your blade is in the water, you'll basically be doing a roll as you pull on the paddle and rotate the boat under your body with your hips. The only difference between the screw-up and the standard roll is that you'll swing your body to the front of the kayak throughout the motions.

Once you can do a screw-up on both sides, I guarantee you'll start using this recovery technique whenever you find your bow falling over-vertical. The trick is to practice it enough so that the motions become natural. If you have to think about what side to screw-up on, then it will probably be too late.

Overview – Screw-ups

- Practice by initiating over-vertical stern squirts on both sides.
- Screw-up/roll in the same direction that you're spinning
- Lead with the head and body, and throw your weight back to grab water with your paddle as soon as possible.
- Swing your weight forward as you rotate the boat underneath your body.

Bow Pirouette

The bow pirouette is a classic playboating move that was developed to spice up the equally classic ender. As you're probably aware, enders aren't nearly as popular nowadays since playboats have shrunk and no longer provide the air time that the long boats did. We're still going to look at bow pirouettes because it is a unique move and a major component of many advanced moves.

The classic bow pirouette is done while performing an ender, though flatwater bow pirouettes are most common with the newer, smaller playboats. Regardless if you're on flatwater, or doing an ender, the way to pirouette off your bow is the same.

Starting with the ender: an ender is initiated in a hole, or on a wave, by driving the bow underwater while pointing to exactly 12 o'clock. The air trapped in your kayak doesn't like being submerged, so it pops back to the surface, sending the kayak into the air, much like a beach ball would. The key to the ender is keeping your kayak pointed to 12 o'clock the whole time, which is accomplished with a steady rudder on one side of the kayak. Once you can consistently perform an ender, you're ready to add the pirouette. There are two ways to initiate your pirouette. The easiest method is using a back sweep. As your bow engages, your rudder remains in the water, keeping your kayak pointed to 12 o'clock. When you start popping up, push the rudder forward to your toes and across the bow. While this lower hand sweeps forward, your top hand and head will lead the way. The top hand does this by punching across the boat, while your head turns aggressively into the spin. Be careful not to land upside down in this position, as your arm will be vulnerable. If you think you're going to land upside down, fight the urge to save yourself with a big high brace, unless of course you enjoy the pain of a dislocated shoulder.

A more difficult method of initiating the pirouette uses the cross-bow draw. This is a more advanced move as you need to maintain your balance while reaching across your kayak for the cross-bow stroke. The cross-bow stroke is basically a forward sweep stroke that you'll reach across the front of your boat to plant. In so doing, you'll have aggressively wound up your body. This cross-bow is the best technique for pirouettes on flatwater. When doing flatwater pirouettes, there are a few things things to keep in mind. First of all, it is very easy to fall past vertical, so try to keep your boat around 60-70 degrees, and don't lean right on the back deck. As you will find out

The back sweep is the easiest method for pirouetting out of a hole. As the paddle sweeps across the bow, the head and top hand lead the way.

in the following chapters, leaning back will actually help pull your kayak past vertical rather than preventing it. Secondly, the cross-bow stroke is a very powerful stroke, so you'll often need to follow up with a backstroke/brace on the other side. Last, but certainly not least, it is once again crucial that you lead the way with your head throughout the move.

The cross-bow draw works best on flatwater. Note the 60-70 degree angle of the kayak and the head leading the way.

After a powerful cross-bow stroke is pulled through, the opposite blade braces to maintain control, while the head continues to lead the way.

Overview – Bow Pirouettes

- *The back sweep technique works best for ender pirouettes.*
- *As you begin popping, push your rudder forward and across your bow, and lead with your head and top hand*
- *Be careful not to land on your paddle with your arms extended.*

- *The cross bow works best on flatwater.*
- *Reach across your boat for a forward sweep.*
- *Lead with the head*
- *Anticipate the need to brace on the opposite side of your stroke.*

BACK DECK ROLL

The back deck roll evolved from the need to roll as quickly as possible, which it helps achieve by skipping the set-up step that both the C-to-C and sweep rolls require. I've heard it said that though it's a quick roll, it's a dangerous roll, as it leaves a paddler's face exposed and puts the shoulder at risk. It's true that your face isn't as well protected, but you spend a LOT less time underwater taunting rocks and your head stays much closer to the surface throughout the roll. With regard to shoulder safety, there is the potential for the shoulder to be put in an awkward position, but if you keep your hands in front of your body and don't overextend your arms, this roll won't pose any more risk than the standard C-to-C or sweep rolls. So when should you use the back deck roll? I use it virtually all the time, and once you learn it, I'm sure it will become your standard roll as well.

The key to the back deck roll is committing yourself to flipping once you've passed the point of no return (the point at which no brace will save you). This commitment involves throwing yourself on the back deck of your kayak and leading the way with your paddle and body. If you can do these two things before you've completely turned upside down, then you can start rolling yourself upright before your kayak has even finished flipping over!

Because of the right-handed offset on most kayak paddles, it's easier to perform the back deck roll flipping to the left, with your right blade doing the work. If you're left-handed and are using a left-control paddle, then you'll want to practice this roll in the opposite direction. Start with your paddle held comfortably in front of your chest, with elbows hanging down and wrists cocked back so that your right paddle blade is facing directly down. You've now formed a rectangle with your arms, paddle and chest. This rectangle should stay relatively intact throughout the roll. Now lean back and aggressively turn your head and upper body to the left. As weird as this sounds, think about trying to kiss the stern end of your kayak! With your head and body aggressively leading the way and your kayak committed to flipping, plant the power face of your left paddle blade at the stern of your boat and slide it under your stern. You can very briefly support some weight on this left blade while your right blade swings towards the back of the boat and enters the water. With your wrists cocked up and the power face down, your right blade will hit the water with

The set-up: wrists cocked back so the power face of the paddle faces down, body and head rotating aggressively to face the stern, and arms held comfortably in front of the body.

a sculling angle that keeps it near the surface. If you've kept your rectangle intact, you should now be lying on the back deck of your kayak, which should be almost completely upside down. This right blade will be providing the support/brace needed to roll the kayak. Continuing to lead the way with your head and body, push your right blade under the stern of your kayak, and then sweep it out to the side. All the while, your wrists remain cocked back to keep the blade near the surface, and your hips roll the kayak upright. The right blade continues on its path all the way to your toes. Still keeping that rectangle between your arms, chest and paddle intact, your body will need to swing forward through the end part of the roll. When your right blade finally reaches your toes, your boat should be completely upright and your body should be in an aggressive position, ready for your next stroke.

Head and body continue to lead the way as the left blade is planted and helps push the stern out of the water. Notice that the rectangle formed by arms, paddle and chest remains intact.

Now lying on the back deck as if trying to 'kiss the stern', the left blade slices under the stern while the right blade hits the water on a sculling angle. The stern is snapped over the body by the hips

The head still leads the way while the right blade continues to sweep a wide arc towards the bow with a sculling angle. This provides constant resistance, which allows the hips to continuously roll the kayak.

The right blade, along with the body, swings to the toes to finish the roll in an aggressive position. Notice the rectangle has kept its form throughout the move.

One of the things that makes the back deck roll so efficient is how quickly you can rotate your torso and throw your body onto the back deck from any position. So, once you're comfortable doing the back deck roll from a normal sitting position, try it while taking various strokes. You'll be amazed at how well it works from any position.

Side Note: The less offset on your paddle, the easier your offside back deck roll will be. This is one reason why I currently use a paddle with virtually no twist.

Finishing the roll by sweeping your body and paddle forward will leave you in an aggressive position, ready for whatever the river throws at you next, or ready to re-establish control if you're in a hole.

Overview – Back Deck Roll

- *For right-handed paddlers, the back deck roll is easiest flipping to the left (rolling up on the right).*
- *Commit to the roll by throwing yourself on the back deck and leading aggressively with head, body and paddle, while maintaining a rectangle with your arms, chest and paddle.*
- *With wrists cocked back so the power faces of your paddle are facing the water, reach to the back of the boat with your paddle and plant the left blade, followed quickly by the right blade.*
- *Keeping the rectangle intact and your wrists cocked, sweep your right blade under your stern and around your kayak, finishing at your toes.*
- *As your paddle sweeps around, roll the boat upright with your hips and knees and finish with your body in an aggressive forward position.*

ENTERING THE WORLD OF VERTICALITY

Practicing any move in a controlled environment is the best way to develop the right technique. Since playboats have shrunk to a point where vertical moves can be performed on flatwater, more and more paddlers are reaching their 'vertical goals'. Does this mean that you should squeeze yourself into the smallest boat possible to practice vertical moves on the flatwater? Absolutely! On flatwater, the smaller the boat one uses, the easier vertical moves will be, and I'm a strong believer that one should learn new skills with the most user-friendly equipment available. Of course, when you're cramming yourself into the smallest playboats there comes a point when the pain factor exceeds the fun and learning factors, so be reasonable!

Whether or not you've got a tiny playboat to practice with, you need to appreciate that vertical moves are going to require a combination of technique and power. Neither on its own will do the trick! We'll start by looking at one of the most basic advanced skills, called the double pump. The double pump is a technique used to throw the bow underwater, which is necessary for the initiation of most advanced moves.

EJ...being EJ

The Double Pimp / Bow Windup

The idea of the double pump is to pull your bow into the air so you have more energy to throw it down into the water. To pull your bow into the air (often referred to as 'winding up the bow'), there are 3 things that you need to do at the same time: tilt your kayak on edge, shift your weight slightly back, and take a forward sweep stroke. Once your bow is in the air, don't hesitate before throwing it down. The power you'll need to throw your bow underwater can only be found through torso rotation. Plant a backstroke just behind your hip and turn your whole upper body so your chest faces the water. Now, as you push on the paddle, throw your weight aggressively forward and unwind your body by pulling your feet down with your knees and stomach muscles.

With boat tilted and weight slightly back, pull down on a sweep stroke to get the bow in the air.

Shoulder Line

The power to force the bow down comes from torso rotation. Note how much the torso is leading the bow.

Here's a drill that focuses on getting your legs and stomach muscles involved with the move. This drill involves alternately sinking your bow and stern, and is commonly referred to as the bobbing drill. You'll start it just as you started the double pump, but once your bow is in the air, don't commit as aggressively to throwing your bow underwater. As your forward sweep turns into a backstroke, shift your weight into a neutral position instead of throwing your weight hard forward. Your body should remain in the neutral position from this point on. You'll now use your knees and stomach muscles to pull your bow (feet) downwards. Once the bow is underwater, turn your backstroke into a forward stroke and pull the bow upwards. Continue to bob your bow in and out of the water about 10 times in total. The key to this drill is taking very short and powerful strokes with your blade completely in the water. You also need to have the balance to hold a steady tilt on your kayak while your stomach muscles work overtime to pull your legs up and down. Since your body stays in a neutral position, your stomach muscles will be doing ALL the work. It shouldn't take too many of these bobs to get your abs burning! You

Keep in mind that the goal of this drill is not to sink your bow and stern as deeply as possible! The goal is to feel your knees and stomach muscles pulling your bow up and down.

Ruth Gordon

might find that after a couple of bobs, your paddle gets caught under your boat and then pulls you upside down. To prevent your paddle from diving, use a sculling angle for every stroke. This means curling your wrists slightly forward as you take a backstroke and cocking your wrists slightly back as you take a forward stroke. This will keep your paddle about a foot or two to the side of your hip and knee, and near the surface.

Overview – Double Pump

Double Pump
- *To 'wind up the bow', simultaneously tilt your boat on edge, shift your weight back and take a forward sweep.*
- *Immediately throw the bow downwards by planting a backstroke just behind the hip, leading aggressively with the head and body and throwing your weight forward.*

Bobbing Drill
- Keep the body as neutral as possible, focusing on the use of the knees and stomach muscles to pull the bow up and down.
- Use very short and powerful strokes with a sculling angle to prevent your paddle from sinking.
- Practice on BOTH sides!

FLATWATER CARTWHEELS

The flatwater cartwheel is a staple playboating move and a major goal for many paddlers. The flatwater cartwheel demonstrates a high level of comfort, balance, and power, as well as an understanding of edge control. With that said, if a big enough, experienced paddler squeezes into a small enough boat, he or she will be throwing flatwater ends fairly quickly. This doesn't mean that the right technique is being used. There is a clear difference between a quality flatwater cartwheel and a muscled flatwater cartwheel. The quality cartwheel will resemble the spinning of an actual wheel. With the body acting as the axle, the boat will revolve at a fairly constant rate. A muscled cartwheel will act more like a wheel with a couple of flat sides. The rotation will stall out after each end as the paddler "hits the wall". Spin momentum then has to be re-established for every end. The best way of looking at a quality flatwater cartwheel is as an aggressive combination of the bow and stern pivot turns. So if you haven't started practicing those pivot turns, you now have another great reason to do so!

So what's the key to the pivot turns again? The key is having the fine edge control to maintain your spin momentum, which means not hitting the wall. The same goes for the flatwater cartwheel. The key to a quality cartwheel is keeping the upper body quiet and making smooth edge transitions that allow you to maintain your spin momentum. Don't expect to make vertical cartwheels either. The ideal flatwater cartwheel is in fact less than vertical and closer to 70 degrees. At this lower angle you can keep your weight over the kayak and stay balanced throughout the move.

The flatwater cartwheel is initiated with the basic double pump technique that we just covered, though you'll need to do so with enough power to bring your bow right underneath your body. Initiating this move with a little forward speed will make it easier to throw the bow down. As we already discussed, the power you'll need to force your bow underwater can only be found through torso rotation. Once you've wound up your bow, turn your whole upper body so your chest faces the water and plant a backstroke just behind your hip. You now unwind your body by pushing off the paddle, throwing your weight forward and pulling your feet downwards with your knees and your stomach muscles. As a rule of thumb, your

As your initiation stroke ends, you boat is levelled off to maintain your spin momentum.

As your stern hits the water, a forward sweep will help pull your bow into the air.

hands should always stay in front of your shoulders, in what we call the 'power position' (see the 'Shoulder Safety' segment). This will keep your shoulders in a safe position and force your body to rotate for any strokes behind your hip. Going back to the bow pivot turn technique, you should know that in order to keep spin momentum going it is crucial that you level off your kayak before your backstroke has finished. For the cartwheel, you'll want to continue past level with this edge transition and tilt your boat in the other direction. Your bow will now charge up toward the water surface while your stern falls downward. As the stern drops to the water, you should be preparing for a stern pivot turn. Since you already have so much spin momentum, you shouldn't need to lean back to help sink your stern. In fact, it is best to keep your upper body in a moderately aggressive position and as quiet as possible. The key is to continue leading the way with your head and upper body, staying ahead of your kayak's progression. As your stern hits the water, you should have a forward sweep stroke already planted at your toes that will help pull your bow into the air. Before your sweep has finished, be sure you have levelled off your kayak and started tilting your boat in the other direction. Once again, lead with your head and body, plant a backstroke and pull your bow underwater with the help of your knees and stomach muscles.

One of the most common problems paddlers have when flatwater

Recognize the stern pivot turn?

When the bow passes vertical you're back at square one. Lead with head and body and pull your bow under with a back stroke.

cartwheeling is falling over vertical. If you find this happening, keep working on your pivot turns, making sure that you're not hitting the wall. If you hit the wall when throwing your kayak down at a 60-90 degree angle, you'll usually end up falling on your face. If you are confident that you are indeed making smooth edge transitions and not hitting the wall, then consider your body position. When your bow is underwater, are you keeping your weight forward? When upright on the bow, the natural tendency is to stand up on the foot braces and lean back. Believe it or not, leaning back actually causes your kayak to pass vertical, so keep your weight forward. We'll look at this in more detail in the bow and stern stalling segments.

Overview – Flatwater Cartwheel

- *The flatwater cartwheel is simply a combination of elevated stern and bow pivot turns.*
- *Initiate with a double pump and aggressively lead the way with the head and body.*
- *Before each stroke has finished, make sure you have made the transition to the next edge.*
- *Keep your weight forward as much as possible, and continue to lead the way with your head and body.*

BOW STALLS

Bow stalling means balancing on the bow of your kayak. This requires awesome balance and control, and is a great move to practice because it forces you to learn the vertical balance points of your kayak.

Like any other vertical move, bow stalling is easiest with the smallest kayaks. So, the smaller the boat you practice this with, the more quickly you'll see results.

The bow stall starts with the basic flatwater cartwheel. Let's look at this move after having initiated a flatwater cartwheel to the right. After initiating the cartwheel with a double pump, you need to stop

your spin momentum when your kayak reaches vertical (from the face on view). The best way to stop your spin momentum is to put on the brakes, which is done with a low brace. In the case of the right side cartwheel, you'll be putting on the brakes with your left paddle blade. Once stalled, you need to stay balanced on end. This balance will require much practice, though you can save yourself a lot of time by understanding what the ideal bow stall position is, and how to make the small corrections that will be necessary to maintain this position.

The ideal bow stall position has your kayak at around a 70-80 degree angle (profile), your body in a moderately aggressive position (which keeps your centre of gravity low), and your paddle completely in the water, in a low brace position, and as far from your kayak as comfortable. To understand this position, picture the kayak and the individual paddle blades as forming the three points of a tripod. The further these points are from each other, the more stable your tripod will be. Of course you can't change the distance between your paddle blades (except by using a longer paddle), but you can modify the distance between your paddle blades and your kayak by reaching further out in front of you.

Though this is the ideal bow stall position, odds are that you'll need to constantly make small adjustments to maintain it. The better you get at stalling, the smaller the adjustments you'll be making. There are three ways that your bow stall can fall apart: your bow will slice up to the surface at the sides, your boat will flatten out, or you'll fall over on your face. To stop your bow from slicing out to the side, you'll be constantly pulling and pushing on your paddle blades. Your paddle will also come in handy when you need to stop yourself from falling on your face, or flattening out. If you're falling forward onto your face you can push out with both paddle blades, in a low-brace position. If you start flattening out, you can actually take a dual forward stroke to pull your boat more vertical by pulling both paddle

Leaning back in a bow stall brings your kayak more vertical.

Leaning forward in a bow stall flattens out your kayak.

blades into the body. It should be noted that all these solutions involve having your whole paddle completely in the water. Though your paddle's activity is important, it won't provide you with enough corrective power on its own. You need to get your whole body into the act by pulling your weight forward or throwing it back. The effect of these different body leans is one of the most misunderstood concepts, and comes into play anytime you're standing on your bow. If you're balancing on your bow and feel yourself falling forward and upside down, the natural thing to do is to lean back in order to prevent yourself from face planting. Believe it or not, this is exactly what NOT to do! Leaning back will actually take you more vertical, while leaning forward will help flatten out your kayak. So next time you feel yourself falling forward while cartwheeling or bow stalling, get your weight forward.

The body leans and the braces that you use will only allow you to recover so much. You'll often pass the point of no return, where no amount of correction can save your stall. With that said, your margin for recovery is directly related to the size of your kayak. The smaller your kayak, the more time you have to recover. This is why practicing in a small boat will let you learn the bow stall much more quickly. It will also be VERY helpful to use a paddle with a very small amount of twist, or with no twist at all, as you'll be able to effectively use both blades at the same time. However, equipment will only help you so much. Keep on practicing and remember that this is one of the trickiest moves to master, but once you find that balance point, it's yours for good!

Overview – Bow Stall

- *Initiate the cartwheel, then hit the brakes with a low brace when you reach vertical.*
- *Set up a tripod with your whole paddle underwater, and as far out from your kayak as comfortable.*
- *Push and pull on your individual paddle blades for lateral stability.*
- *Lean forward and push on a dual low brace to flatten out.*
- *Lean back and take a dual forward stroke to pull yourself more vertical.*

STERN STALLS

The stern stall involves balancing your kayak on its stern end and facing towards the sky. Before working on the stern stall, I would recommend that you first figure out the bow stall, to get the feel for balancing on end. Either way, expect this move to take LOTS of practice.

There are a few ways of getting yourself into a vertical stern stall position. You can do a standard flatwater cartwheel and stop your spin momentum on the 2nd end with a brake, you can stern squirt your bow into the air, or you can simply start with a stern initiated flatwater cartwheel. The stern initiated cartwheel is the most straightforward technique, so this is the one that we're going to look at. To initiate your stern on flatwater you're going to need to double pump your stern, just as you double pumped your bow. This means pulling your stern into the air so that you'll have more energy to throw it down. As with the bow double pump, initiating this move with a little speed will make it easier. Being the exact opposite of winding up your bow, you'll double pump your stern by taking a back stroke while tilting your boat aggressively into the stroke and throwing your weight forward. Doing this, you should be able to effectively force your bow down and push your stern into the air. Then, with your boat kept on the same steep edge, aggressively lead with your head and body, take a powerful forward sweep stroke, and throw your weight back to sink your stern underwater. This stern initiation can actually be a bit easier than the bow initiation since you're using a powerful forward stroke to pull your bow into the air, and the sterns of playboats are smaller than the bows. With a well-timed reverse double pump, you should be able to pull your bow into the air quite smoothly. As your bow reaches vertical, you're ready to put on the brakes and stall out your cartwheel. Putting on the brakes in a stern stall position is simply a matter of using a high brace, which in the case of a cartwheel to the right, would be done with the power face of the right blade.

Now that you've stalled yourself in the vertical position, we'll look at how to stay balanced like this. As we did with the bow stall, we'll look at the ideal stern stall position, and then look at how to make the small adjustments needed to maintain it. The ideal stern stall position has your kayak just off vertical (between 80 and 85 degrees), with your back flat against the water, and your arms over your head with both paddle blades lying in the water. Similar to the bow stall, your paddle blades and kayak form a tripod for balance. Stretching your arms over your head could potentially stress your shoulders if you were to try to use your paddle blades too aggressively, but it is important to get your paddle as far away from your kayak as you comfortably can in order to establish the most balanced tripod. Maintaining this stable stern stall position will require constant adjustments, but of course the better you get at it, the smaller the adjustments you'll need. There are three ways that you can lose control of your stern stall: your stern can slice out the side, your boat can flatten out, or your bow can fall over top of you. As with the bow stall, your paddle and body need to work together to prevent all of these things from happening. Unlike the bow stall though, your paddle stays on the surface, so it can't play as active a role. You'll need to rely more on your body positioning. By pushing against the water with the backside of your paddle blades, you should be able to effectively stabilize yourself laterally and you should be able to

Reverse double pump your bow into the air, then put on the brakes and get your paddle over your head.

stop your kayak from falling over top of you. The problem is that you can't pull up on the water to stop your kayak from flattening out. This means you'll need to rely on keeping your bow up with your stomach muscles. To keep your boat from flattening out, lean forward and pull your legs to your chest. This will be very effective in bringing your kayak vertical and will give your abs a wicked workout! You'll need to be careful that you don't pull your boat too vertical. If your boat begins falling over vertical, then lean back and push your legs away from your body, while pushing against the water with the backsides of your paddle blades. This has the effect of flattening out your kayak.

Lean back and push your legs away to flatten out your kayak.

Lean forward and pull your knees to your chest to bring your kayak more vertical.

The only way to nail the stern stall is to practice until your recoveries and adjustments become natural. If you need to think about which way to lean, you'll more than likely pass the point of no return. Like the bow stall, this move is easiest with the smallest boats and with a paddle with minimal twist so that both blades can be used at the same time. Personally, I found the stern stall to be one of the trickiest moves to master, but since finding the balance point, the stern stall has been one of my favourite moves.

Overview – Stern Stall

- Initiate the stern with a reverse double pump, then hit the brakes with a high brace to stall your boat at the vertical position.
- Set up a tripod with your paddle on the surface with arms outstretched over your head.
- Brace with the backside of your individual paddle blades for lateral stability.
- Lean forward and pull your legs to your chest to go more vertical.
- Lean back and push with the backside of your paddle blades to flatten out.

Party Trick

The party trick is a very powerful flatwater move that involves moving from an upside down position directly into a bow stall. Like many play moves, the party trick doesn't really have a whitewater application. It's simply a cool move to learn! To even consider trying this move, you'll need a boat that's small enough to throw around on flatwater with relative ease, because it requires you to throw a flatwater cartwheel without any type of bow wind-up.

Let's start by looking at the set-up position. This is the position you'll start from once you're upside down. I'll leave the flipping part up to you… If you've got a stronger side for cartwheels (as most paddlers do) then you'll want to use that side for this move. For a left-side cartwheel your body will lean out to the right, and for a right-side cartwheel your body will lean out to the left. The set-up position involves lying back and leaning right out to the side, with your whole upper body facing the bottom of the river. Your paddle should be in front of your face and parallel to your kayak, with the non-power face sides of your paddle facing down. Now pull your arms towards you so that your paddle is only inches from your nose. This is the set-up position.

From the set-up position, the party trick involves two separate actions that are combined to appear like a single motion. First, you need to get your kayak onto edge so that you can slice the bow underwater. Once your boat is on edge, you need to pull your bow underwater using a powerful back initiation stroke. The trickiest part of this move is getting enough power from your paddle to pull the bow right down. With that said, it should make sense that you don't want to lose any of your paddle's

The set-up position: leaning back and out to side, facing downward, with paddle just in front of the face and parallel to the kayak.

potential power while getting your boat on edge. So then how do you get your boat on edge? The power required to get your boat on edge comes from pushing your whole paddle down, out and away from your body. This is why you set up with your paddle pulled close to your face. With your kayak on edge, it's time to pull your bow down. Like the standard flatwater cartwheel, you'll do this by taking a powerful back sweep, throwing your weight forward, and pulling your bow downward with your knees and stomach muscles. Once the bow is down, you'll be using the same bow stalling technique that we just covered. One thing to keep in mind is that it is very common to end up falling past vertical when trying this move. To compensate for this, you'll want to throw your weight as far forward as possible while you pull your bow downwards.

Overview – Party Trick

- Set-up position: lean back and out to the side while facing the river bottom. The paddle is held close in front of your face, parallel to your kayak and in the low-brace position
- Step 1: get your boat on edge by pushing out and away with the whole paddle.
- Step 2: with your boat on edge, back sweep, throw your weight forward, and pull your bow downward.
- Stabilize in the bow stall position.

Pushing your paddle down and away from your body provides the leverage needed to roll the kayak on edge, without using up power from your back sweep. With boat on edge and body wound up, pull the bow down with standard flatwater cartwheeling technique.

Zero-to-Hero

The zero-to-hero is a lot like the party trick, as it involves moving from the upside down position (zero), to a stern stall (hero). Not surprisingly, this move requires a lot of power and a very small boat. You also need to be comfortable with flatwater cartwheels and stern stalls.

As always, we'll start by looking at the set-up position. The set-up for the zero-to-hero is basically the same as that for a C-to-C roll. You need to get a paddle blade near the surface out at 90 degrees to your kayak. Like the party trick, there are two steps to the zero-to-hero. First you need to get your boat on edge, and then you need to pull your bow into the air. To roll your boat on edge, you'll get the purchase from your paddle by cocking your wrists back slightly and sculling your paddle towards your toes. As you roll your boat on edge, your paddle turns into a 'heroically' powerful forward sweep stroke that pulls directly downward on the water. With the help of your stomach muscles, this sweep stroke should pull your bow vertically into the air. You then need to stabilize yourself in a stern stall, which means putting on the brakes and getting your paddle over your head to set up the tripod.

Pulling your paddle to your toes across the water surface will provide that little bit of leverage needed to roll your kayak on edge.

As your kayak rolls on edge, pull the stern down hard with a forward sweep. Be careful not to roll the kayak too far on edge, or you'll end up doing a normal roll.

Once your bow is vertical, put on the brakes with a stroke on the other side, and get your paddle above your head to stabilize in a stern stall.

Overview – Zero-to-Hero

- Set-up position: standard C-to-C roll position with paddle blade near the surface at 90 degrees to the kayak.
- Scull your blade toward your toes to get the purchase necessary for rolling your boat on edge.
- As your boat rolls on edge, take a super powerful sweep stroke to pull your bow vertically into the air.
- Put on the brakes and stabilize yourself in the stern stall position

Wave
Moves

The clean air blunt - Corran Addison

FRONT SURFING

Front surfing is without a doubt one of the coolest feelings in the world. There's nothing quite like sitting on a wave and watching the water fly by your kayak. For those who have never surfed before, we'll start by looking at the basics that will let you catch your first wave. For those of you who surf, but find yourselves regularly getting blown off waves, we'll look at a front surfing technique that will help keep you where you want to be. Lastly, we'll look at an aggressive front surfing technique that will let experienced surfers take full advantage of the steepest, fastest waves, as well as breaking waves and holes.

There really are very few sensations like carving across the face of a wave, watching the water fly by your kayak.

Catching Waves

Catching a wave is often a novice wave surfer's biggest challenge. You have two viable options. You can catch a wave on the fly, or you can ferry onto a wave from a nearby eddy. Ferrying from an abutting eddy is the easier method because you don't have downstream momentum trying to take you up and over the wave. So let's look at this technique first.

The trick to ferrying onto a wave is deciding on, then following, a plan of action that allows you to slide onto the wave while ideally staying on its face the whole time. Staying on the face of the wave allows gravity to keep you where you want to be, and you won't have to worry as much about your bow diving underwater. Entering too far upstream places you in the fastest moving water as it rushes downhill towards the wave. As you slide back onto the wave you can easily end up with enough downstream momentum to carry you up and completely over the wave. You'll also have to worry about having your bow catch water as your boat passes through the dip at the wave's trough. In order to successfully stay on the wave's face, you'll need to consider your kayak's angle, speed, and its point of entry into the current.

As every wave is different, and the speeds of the main current can vary greatly, there's no cut-and-dry way of catching a wave However, there are a few key things to keep in mind. Firstly, aim to keep your

When ferrying onto a wave from an eddy, choose an approach that slides you across the face of the wave, never letting your bow upstream of the wave's trough.

Trough

bow at, or downstream of, the wave's trough. This will keep your boat on the wave's face. Secondly, the faster the water is moving, the more upstream angle you'll need when entering the current. If in doubt, you're better off having too much upstream angle because it's easier to let your angle go than to recover a lost angle.

Dropping onto a wave from upstream requires more finesse and power. The toughest part of dropping in is lining up to catch the steepest part of the wave. You need to effectively read the water flowing into the wave to decide on the best path. As you near the wave, slow yourself down as much as possible with powerful forward strokes. If the wave you're trying to catch is steep, you'll need to lean back when you reach the trough of the wave to help prevent your bow from diving. As soon as your bow is clear, lean forward aggressively to stay on the wave. If the wave isn't too steep, you can stay in a moderately aggressive position the whole time.

When dropping onto a wave, keep an eye on where you're going and slow yourself down with powerful forward strokes

As you reach the trough of the wave, keep your weight back a bit to prevent your bow from catching water.

As soon as you're past the trough and on the face of the wave, get your weight forward and take some powerful forward strokes to stop all your downstream momentum.

The Surf Zone

So you've caught the wave. Now let's look at how to stay there…

Playboats are being designed to surf waves incredibly well. Their flat hulls and sharp edges make them highly responsive, but it is the length of today's playboats that has really opened up the number of surfable waves on the river. Short playboats may not have the hull speed to surf the low-angle waves that longer boats can sit on, but they can surf smaller, steeper, and more dynamic waves. They are also much more forgiving to paddle, so you'll be able to sit quite passively on many waves without necessarily having to use perfect technique. That's great, but we're interested in developing the proper surfing techniques that will set you up for more advanced moves down the road.

First of all, you've got to understand that all your surf time should be spent on the face of a wave. The only effective way of keeping your kayak there on the mellower waves is by carving back and forth from one ferry angle to the next. Let's look at how the body, paddle and boat are involved in making this happen.

Body Position: Though you'll often need to lean back to keep your bow from diving, remember that your weight should be kept forward as much as possible. When sitting upright you're more stable, have more control over boat tilts, and are in the position necessary for initiating more advanced moves. With that said, don't lock yourself into any one position. Feel free to be active with your forward and backward leans. If you're sliding into the trough of the wave and your bow is diving, it's all right to lean back. If you're falling off the backside of the wave, then lean aggressively forward.

The Paddle: Your paddle should be acting as a rudder whenever possible. The rudder is your kayak's steering wheel. If it's not in the water, you're not in control. Plant the rudder with your paddle parallel to your kayak and with your front hand held between shoulder and eye level. Keeping your front hand high like this sets your active blade deep in the water. Having your paddle parallel to the kayak will ensure that the rudder is not acting as a brake. Though braking rudders can be useful in aggressive surfing situations, they will often pull you off the smaller waves. Your chest/belly button should   be turned to face your paddle. This winds up your body so that your

Don't be afraid to be active with your forward and backward leans. If you're falling off the backside of the wave, lean forward.

rudder can act as a pivot, allowing your stomach muscles to help pull the bow around. Turning your chest toward your paddle shaft also keeps your hands in front of your body which, as you already know, protects your shoulders. Holding your elbows down will also keep your shoulders in the safest position. From this ruddering position you can turn your boat in either direction by simply turning your wrists. By rotating your wrists upward, you'll catch water with the

A good rudder is planted at the stern with the body wound up, the elbows down, and the front hand between shoulder and eye level.

power face of your blade and draw your stern towards your paddle. By curling your wrists slightly downward, the back face of your paddle will catch water and pry your stern away from your paddle. You can get a good feel for both the stern draw and stern pry on flatwater with the following drill. Establish some forward speed, then start coasting with a rudder in the water that keeps you going straight.

Without moving your arms, try rotating your wrists both up and down and feel the pressure moving from one face of the paddle blade to the next. You will find that prying your stern away from your paddle (curling wrists down) is an easier and much more powerful action. This is why you'll usually be switching back and forth, using rudders on both sides of your kayak when surfing. When doing this, you're alternating from one stern pry to the next. Each pry is responsible for holding your ferry angle and cutting your kayak back into the other direction when the time comes.

The Boat: Your boat will be in one of two positions. It will either be facing directly upstream (12 o'clock), or it will be on a ferry angle. When pointed to 12 o'clock your kayak wants to shoot down into the trough of the wave, so unless you're on a fairly flat wave, you'll want to spend all your time alternating from one ferry angle to the other. So which way should you edge your kayak? On flatter, smooth waves you can tilt your boat slightly into each turn without worrying about catching your upstream edge. As the waves get steeper and you begin carving back and forth more aggressively, it becomes more important to keep your kayak tilted downstream so that your upstream edge doesn't get caught. This is what the aggressive front surfing section deals with.

1. With wrists curled down, the backside of the paddle catches water and will pry the stern away from the paddle.

2. With wrists cocked back, the power face catches water and will draw the stern to the paddle.

For the braking rudder, the paddle is held in front of the body so that it catches a lot of water.

Aggressive Surfing

By carving back and forth, you'll be able to stay on the face of a mellow wave, but surfing gets considerably tougher when waves get steeper or start breaking, as you'll be pulled into the trough more forcefully. When this happens you need to use an aggressive surfing technique. The ultimate goal remains the same: stay out of the wave's trough. There are two techniques that you can use to do this. You can balance your kayak at the top of the wave, or cut back and forth aggressively across the face of the wave.

Balancing on top of a wave is very tricky because it's easy to fall off the backside. It's an important skill to learn though, as it's a great technique for setting up advanced moves. In order to stay at the top of a wave you'll need to have a great feel for surfing because it will require quick and constant adjustments. You'll also need to use a braking stroke. The braking stroke is a rudder that acts like a backstroke to prevent you from sliding down into the trough. Instead of your paddle being parallel to your kayak, your paddle will be held just in front of your body and will be planted beside your hip. You'll need to alternate between braking strokes, as each one will turn your boat.

The most effective way to deal with a steep or breaking wave is by aggressively carving across its face. The key to this technique is moving from one strong ferry angle to another, spending the least amount of time pointing to 12 o'clock. Whenever your bow is pointed to 12 o'clock it is much more likely to dive underwater and your kayak will have the strongest urge to shoot down into the trough of the wave. Carving aggressively requires a real commitment to your rudder. As you carve in one direction, your rudder should be planted deeply on the upstream side of your kayak with your chest turned to face directly upstream. Keeping your front hand high will help you get the active blade as deep in the water as possible. As for your boat, you must prevent your upstream edge from catching. To do this, you'll need to tilt your kayak downstream, away from your rudder. This means shifting your weight to the butt cheek furthest from your rudder. This is the same tilt that you would use when ferrying across a wave. Your kayak should be on edge enough so that your boat is carving its course, but don't try to carve too aggressively. The more on edge that your boat is, the more you'll fight to maintain your ferry angle and the less balanced you'll be. With this technique, you'll be able to carve across the face of any wave with an awesome ferry angle while your shoulders stay square with the main current.

When you want to cut back in the other direction, the shoulder of the wave is usually your best bet because it's not quite as steep as the face. Cutting back is simply a matter of pulling your bow around with your stomach and knees as you push on a powerful stern pry. As your bow sweeps around to 12 o'clock, start flattening out the tilt

Aggressively carving across the face of a wave: weight is on the downstream butt cheek, rudder planted deeply on the upstream side with the body wound up. Notice the stern is kept under the foam pile, keeping the bow in the air.

on your boat. When your bow reaches 12 o'clock your boat should be flat, and then should continue to tilt in the other direction as you pass 12 o'clock. Remember that you want to spend the least amount of time possible pointing to 12 o'clock.

To cut back in the other direction, pry hard on your rudder and pull your bow around with your stomach and knees, while gradually leveling your boat tilt so that your boat is flat when it reaches 12 o'clock. Don't stop at 12 o'clock!

The aggressive carving technique is a great way to surf most of the waves you'll encounter on the river. Keep in mind that just because it's called the 'aggressive technique', that doesn't mean that it can only be used on the most aggressive waves. Any wave that tends to catch your bow is a good candidate for this type of surfing. This is also one of the best ways to get out of the trough of a hole in order to set up advanced moves on top of the pile. But we'll get into that later on....

Recoveries

No matter how good you get at front surfing, your bow will dive underwater every once in a while. To recover from this, quickly and briefly tilt your kayak on edge. This temporarily relieves the water pressure on your bow, allowing it to resurface.

FLAT SPINS

The flat spin is a move that flat-hulled kayaks have made possible. Playboats are now being designed to be as 'loose', or slippery as possible, which means they flat spin incredibly well. In fact, they do such a good job of it, that paddlers sometimes find themselves spinning out of control. The reality is that if you're surfing on a big fast wave, it won't take 'perfect' technique to get your kayak spinning. However, when you're on smaller, more technical waves, you'll be forced to use the optimal technique. It is this technique that we're going to look at, because it will take you a step closer to the advanced play moves.

We're going to look at three separate components of this move: the set-up, the initiation and the recovery.

Firstly, you need to understand that when you spin on a wave, your kayak catches water and will tend to be pulled downstream. This means that you need to follow a plan of action that will keep you on the face of the wave and prevent you from being pulled right off. Consider the form of a wave: the wave is steepest at the peak and then gradually flattens out as you move towards the trough. This means that gravity will be most helpful in this regard high up on the wave face, rather than in the trough. It should then make sense that the ideal spot to initiate a flat spin is high up on the face of the steepest part of a wave. It is also important that you have some upstream momentum. This prevents your kayak from being pulled downstream as soon as you start spinning.

The best way to get positioned at the top of a wave is to carve your way up, or to pull yourself downstream with braking strokes. Once you're in position, point your kayak to 12 o'clock and let yourself begin to slide down into the trough. Just as you feel yourself starting to drop down the face of the wave, it's time to initiate the spin with a back sweep, while keeping your boat flat to the water. It's very important that you understand what you need your kayak to do during the flat spin. When you're front surfing on a wave, the stern edges of your kayak are actively working in the water, while your bow edges are often completely out of the water. To spin, you need to release these stern edges; otherwise, your kayak will want to continue to carve. To release the stern edges, throw your weight forward and push down on your back sweep at the same time that you push away with it. Now, if you can establish spin momen--tum, then you'll be able to flat spin on almost any surfable wave. Let's look at this move from the beginning…. You make your way to the top of the wave and just as you start sliding down the face of the wave, you initiate the spin. Lead with your head and body and plant your paddle firmly out to the side and just behind your hip. Push down and away with your paddle, aggressively pull your bow towards that active blade, and throw your weight forward to lift your stern. Recognize the bow pivot turn? The only issue left to address is the edging of the kayak. As was mentioned before, big, fast waves are easy to spin on since the kayak will literally be skipping across the surface. Smaller waves are more difficult to spin on, and therefore require a more aggressive technique. Looking back to the basic bow pivot turn, we tilted our kayak into our back sweep to force the bow underwater and push the stern into the air. Though the goal of the flat spin is not necessarily to force the bow underwater, it is definitely crucial that you pop the stern out of the water. With that said, the edging you'll use for the flat spin is very similar to that of the bow pivot turn, but less aggressive. As you initiate the spin with a back sweep, tilt your boat slightly downstream, into your sweep stroke. This tilt should be enough to pop your stern edges out of the water, but no more. The flatter you can keep your kayak, the better. Now, just as with the bow pivot turn, the success of your spin is reliant on your ability to level off your boat tilt before your stroke has finished. If you find yourself carving off the wave instead of spinning around, then either you haven't popped your stern edges completely out of the water, or you over-tilted your kayak.

By pushing down and away with a back sweep, snapping your weight forward, and tilting your boat slightly downstream, you will release your stern edges and let your boat spin around a point between your feet and knees.

On small waves, you'll often have to finish your 180-degree spin with a recovery stroke so that you don't get swept off the wave. The

With a little upstream momentum, initiate the spin from back to front with a forward sweep and your head and body leading the way. Recognize the basic stern pivot turn?

By pulling down with your sweep, tilting your boat slightly downstream, and snapping your weight back, you can lift your bow edges out of the water, and pivot around a point behind your butt.

The recovery stroke is a follow-up stroke on the other side of the boat that kills your spin momentum and keeps you on the wave.

recovery stroke is a backstroke taken on the opposite side of the kayak from your initiating back sweep. This backstroke will help keep you on the wave and will help you establish control in a back surf. Establishing control in the back surf is important, because going for a full 360 will usually pull you right off the small waves. You'll need to stop, get repositioned at the peak of the wave and then spin back around. As you can imagine, getting set up in a back surf will require great back surfing awareness and this only comes through practice. Practice back surfing, back paddling, eddy turns, ferries, etc… Anything that you can do forward, you should ultimately be able to do in reverse!

Spinning from a back surf to a front surf is very similar to the first part of the spin. You'll need to initiate on the steepest part of the wave, with a slight bit of upstream momentum. Lead the spin with your head and body, plant your paddle at your toes and use your stomach muscles to pull the bow around. This time, you'll need to release your bow edges, so throw your weight back as you initiate the spin, while keeping your hull flat to the water. Recognize the pivot turn technique? The flat spin is simply a low-angle pivot turn on the face of a wave! Once again, the small waves will require you to finish with a recovery stroke, which will be a forward stroke on the opposite side of the kayak to your initiation stroke.

Full 360 Spin

To do a full 360-degree flat spin and maintain your surf, you'll need a decent-sized wave, or a wave that is breaking enough to hold you there. The key to the full 360-degree spin is initiating as much spin

Overview - Flat Spins

- *Set up high on the face of the steepest part of a wave and initiate with slight upstream momentum.*
- *Initiate with a sweep, a snappy weight transition, and your boat tilted downstream enough to pop your end out of the water, but no more.*
- *Finish with a recovery stroke to re-establish control after each 180 spin.*

momentum as possible with the first stroke, then keeping it going. Maintaining your spin momentum requires having an active paddle in the water, from which you can continue to pull your boat around. This means that once your first stroke is done and your boat has been levelled out, your next blade gets planted as quickly as possible, at which time your boat is tilted slightly downstream once again. The quickest way of getting your next stroke in the water is by dropping it in at your hip or knee. You won't get the most pull from a stroke that is planted so close to your body, but with spin momentum already established, it is more important to just get a pivot blade in the water than to take any extra time to reach for a more powerful stroke at your toes. With this second stroke in the water, you can continue to pull your bow around with your knees and stomach muscles. To make it around in a full 360, you'll also need to make smooth and timely weight transitions. This means throwing your weight forward for the first part of the spin and then shifting it back for the second part of the spin. Finally, it's important to understand what the head does throughout this move. Ideally, your eyes stay upstream as much as possible, as this is where the water would catch you off guard. On bigger waves, it is reasonable to keep your eyes upstream right up until the point that you plant your second stroke. At that time, your head turns and looks upstream over the shoulder, and once again leads the way. On smaller waves, when you need the utmost in power, you're better off leading with your head the whole way through the spin. In this case,

On fast waves, the eyes can look upstream until the second stroke is planted. Notice the second stroke being planted between the hip and knee; A less powerful, but quick stroke.

With the second stroke planted deeply, the knees and stomach muscles can continue to pull the bow around, while the head turns and once again leads the way.

you are trading general awareness for added power, but it is an essential compromise. Eventually, when you can combine a powerful initiation, good weight transfer, and minimal edging, you'll find that you won't even need a second stroke to get yourself around… and so emerges the clean spin!

Overview - Full 360's

- *The Full 360 will only work on a decent-sized wave, or a wave that is breaking.*
- *Initiate just as you would a 180-degree spin, only with more power.*
- *Once your first stroke finishes, drop your next stroke into the water as quickly as possible.*
- *Keep your eyes upstream as much as possible, though on smaller waves you'll need to lead with the head.*

Clean / Super Clean Spins

A clean spin is a complete 360-degree flat spin that is done with a single stroke. A super-clean spin is a 540-degree spin done with a single stroke. Though these may sound really difficult, they really aren't that tough! Believe it or not, paddlers have even been known to get clean 1080-degree spins or more. Having the right technique is crucial for any clean spins, but you'll also need the right boat and the right wave.

To begin, you will need a boat with a 'loose' hull, and a good-sized wave. With that said, you'll be amazed at the small size of some of the waves on which the best paddlers can clean spin. This goes to show you that equipment isn't everything. You also need solid technique and power.

Clean spins are initiated in exactly the same way as normal flat spins, though you won't have the same room for error and you'll need all the power you can get from your initiation stroke. This means you'll start at the peak of the wave and as you begin sliding down the face of the wave you'll use a powerful back sweep to release your stern edges.

Once spinning, the success of the clean spin will rely on smooth weight transfers as you lead aggressively with your head and body. Even though you don't have a paddle to pull your boat around, simply leading with your head and body can effectively pull your spins around. As for your body weight transfers, we just looked in detail at how these were applied to flat spins, but to recap: when going from front surf to back surf, you pivot around a point under your knees, so your weight should be forward. When spinning from back surf to front surf, you pivot around a point behind your butt, so your weight should be slightly back. It is important to note that the faster the wave you're surfing, the more effectively your kayak will be planing, and the less effort it will take to release your stern or bow edges. This means that you can keep your body weight more centered on the bigger, faster waves.

So there you have it. With smooth body weight transfers and your head and body aggressively leading the spins, you should be able to clean spin on a wide variety of waves. Like most playboating moves, a large part of your success will come from setting up the move well, so take the time to get to the top of the wave and build some upstream speed.

Overview - Clean / Super Clean Spins

- *Initiate the move like a normal flat spin, making sure you get the most help from the wave by starting at the peak.*
- *Lead aggressively with your head and body.*
- *Make smooth weight transitions. The more effectively your kayak planes, the more centered you can keep your weight.*

Back Surfing

Since the majority of playboating moves involve spinning, you'll be spending almost as much time backward as forward on waves. So doesn't it make sense that you're as comfortable going this way? With that said, back surfing is the most under-practiced playboating skill and a major weakness for many freestyle paddlers. By practicing back surfing, you'll not only develop an important skill for setting up and recovering from moves, but you'll enhance your overall backward awareness which will help your paddling immensely. To prepare yourself for back surfing, work on your backward eddy turns and ferries. You need to reach a level of proficiency where your strokes and boat tilts become natural, because if you have to think about them when you're on a wave, it will invariably be too late!

Catching the wave:

Catching a wave in a back surf is often harder than the actual back surfing! It's often easiest to start in a front surf and spin to a back surf, though you should learn to catch a wave in reverse. Let's start by looking at a good way of back ferrying onto a wave from an abutting eddy. Approach the eddyline slowly, upstream of the wave's trough, pointing forward. Stick your bow into the main current and alllow it to get taken downstream. With the right approach speed, you'll get spun backward on the eddyline and will be taken downstream to the shoulder of the wave. Once you're in line with the wave's shoulder, take a powerful back sweep in the eddy to push your stern onto a ferry angle in the main current. Using a light bow pivot turn here will help you do this. As soon as you've done so, the main current will try to spin your kayak downstream. To prevent this, take a second sweep stroke on the main current side of your kayak, then plant a rudder on the eddy side of your kayak. The trick is entering the main current at the shoulder of the wave, as your stern will stay clear of the oncoming water, and gravity will be working on your side. If you sweep your stern into the current too early, you'll find yourself in the trough of the wave, and are much more likely to get swept downstream.

Dropping onto a wave backwards is no different than doing so forwards. You'll need to decide on an approach that will take you to the steepest part of the wave. As you approach the wave, slow down any downstream momentum with some powerful backstrokes. For steeper waves, you'll need to be watch that your stern doesn't catch water when you reach the trough. You can avoid this by leaning forward and tilting your boat slightly into each stroke. Once past the trough, lean back and continue taking powerful backstrokes, until you've settled on the face of the wave.

Stick your bow into the current upstream of the wave's trough.

At the shoulder, perform a light bow pivot turn with a back sweep in the eddy to push the stern into the current and onto a ferry angle.

The ferry angle is established on the shoulder of the wave.

Control your backsurf with a rudder.

When back ferrying onto a wave, it's easy to peel out of the eddy too high. Keep your eyes on where you're going and stay on the face of the wave.

The Surf Zone:

The rules for back surfing are the same as those for front surfing. Most importantly, you need to stay on the face of the wave. Your boat will be in one of two positions. It will either be facing directly upstream (12 o'clock), or it will be on a ferry angle. When pointed to 12 o'clock your kayak will want to shoot down into the trough of a wave, so unless you're on a fairly flat wave, you'll want to spend your time alternating from one ferry angle to another. As with front surfing, we'll look individually at the roles of your body, paddle and boat.

The Body: Though you should feel free to use any forward or backward lean, there is an ideal body position that should be maintained whenever possible. The ideal back surfing position is a moderately aggressive position (weight slightly forward). We'll refer to this as the 'default' back surfing position. Too often, paddlers will simply kiss their front deck in the hopes of preventing their stern edges from catching. Though this can sometimes keep your surf going, it is a terrible habit to get into. Focus on carving back and forth from one ferry angle to the next. You may find yourself washing off the wave when learning this, but you will be developing the control and awareness necessary for any more advanced move. This will help keep you higher on the face of a wave and will keep your stern edges out of the water.

The Paddle: A proper back surfing rudder is planted somewhere around your feet, with the body wound up. Both elbows should stay low to keep the shoulders safe and the top hand is kept at around shoulder level and held quite close to the body. As the rudder is moved closer to the knees, it will act more as a brake. The closer to the bow the rudder gets planted, the less resistance it will create with the water. Just as with front surfing, on waves that aren't particularly steep you'll find that a rudder that creates less resistance works best, as a braking rudder tends to pull you right off these waves.

The Boat: Don't forget to use the edges of your boat to carve. On flat, or smooth waves, you can tilt your boat slightly into each turn without worrying about catching your upstream edge. As waves get steeper and you begin carving back and forth more aggressively, it becomes important to keep your kayak tilted downstream so that your upstream edge doesn't get caught. This is what the aggressive back surfing section deals with next.

The toughest part about back surfing is keeping track of where you are on the wave. Of course, this awareness comes with practice, but it also helps to take a good look around. Don't get caught with the blinders on! It also helps a great deal to get to know a wave in a front surf first, as you'll figure out where the wave's sweet spots are.

The ideal back surfing position: moderately aggressive body position, low resistance rudder, and staying on the face of the wave.

Don't be afraid to move your body around. If you need to lean back, do so. Just understand that you want to spend as much time as possible in a moderately aggressive position.

Overview - Back Surfing

- Get to know the sweet spots of a wave in a front surf first.
- Stay on the face of the wave by carving back and forth. Don't get caught kissing your front deck in 'survival surf' mode.
- Plant the rudder at your toes with elbows down and with your top hand close to the body and at around shoulder level.
- On the mellowest waves, tilt your boat slightly towards your rudder to help carve turns.

Agressive Surfing:

When waves get steeper, or start breaking, you'll have to use an aggressive back surfing technique, which is basically the reverse of your aggressive front surfing technique. The goal remains staying high on the wave face. The only difference is in the rudder that you use. You've got two options, both of which require you to stay loose at the hips and to commit to your rudder. You can use braking strokes, or you can carve back and forth aggressively on the wave's face. Both techniques are tricky because you'll be working largely by feel, but the aggressive carving method is definitely more reliable because it allows more room for error. The backward, aggressive carving technique involves back ferrying back and forth across the wave face, aggressively enough to keep your stern from diving underwater, while spending the least amount of time pointing to 12 o'clock. The more time you spend at 12 o'clock, the more likely your stern is to dive underwater. As we already mentioned, holding your back ferry will require you to stay loose at the hips and to commit to your rudder. Your rudder gets planted on the upstream side of your kayak, while your kayak is tilted downstream, preventing the upstream edge from catching. When the time comes to cut back in the other direction, make the turn quick and aggressive. This is done by pulling hard on your rudder, as a forward sweep, while maintaining the downstream tilt on your kayak, so your bow is pulled down and your stern is kept in the air. As your stern passes 12 o'clock you need to quickly get your boat onto its other edge, and plant the next rudder so that you can carve across the wave in the other direction.

With your boat tilted downstream, you can pull hard on your rudder and cut back in the other direction, keeping your stern in the air.

When the stern passes 12 o'clock, tilt the boat in the other direction and plant the next rudder.

Braking strokes will come in handy when a wave is super steep, or isn't wide enough to carve across. To make them effective, you'll combine your braking strokes with the aggressive carving technique we just covered. This means tilting your kayak downstream and away from each braking stroke, to lift your stern. The difference is that you're now relying on your paddle blades to provide the resistance to stop your boat from sliding into the trough of the wave. You'll get this resistance by holding your paddle away from your body, perpendicular to the main current. Aggressive back surfing is one of the toughest skills to nail, but once you've figured it out, a world of new moves will be opened to you.

A braking stroke can come in handy if you need to stop yourself from sliding upstream in a hurry.

Overview - Aggressive Back Surfing

Aggressive Carving
- Stay on the face by moving from one ferry angle to the next, spending the least amount of time pointing to 12 o'clock.
- With your kayak tilted downstream, hold your ferry angle with a rudder planted deeply on the upstream side.
- Cut back at the shoulder of the wave by pulling hard on your rudder and keeping your boat tilted downstream. As you pass 12 o'clock, tilt the boat in the other direction and plant the next rudder.

Braking Stroke
- Hold your paddle away from your body and perpendicular to the current to catch the maximum amount of water.
- Combine the braking strokes with your aggressive carving technique.

BLUNTS

The blunt is a radical change from front surf to back surf, in which the stern is thrown almost vertically into the air. This is definitely one of the most dynamic freestyle kayaking moves out there, and though the smallest boats make it possible to throw blunts on all sorts of different waves, the steeper waves always provide the best results.

The blunt requires an aggressive set-up, execution and recovery. If you're weak in any of these departments, your blunt will end up as a 'flop'. So let's look at each of these components individually.

Setting up a blunt is difficult and requires a high level of wave surfing proficiency. The ultimate goal of your set up is to shoot to the wave's shoulder with as much speed as possible. It's important that you stay fairly high on the face, as the lower you are, the more greenwater your bow will catch when you initiate the blunt. To build the most speed, you'll need to start at the peak of the wave. Pointing to the blunt shoulder, get your boat on edge and carve aggressively in that direction. You can also take a power stroke on the downstream side for an added forward boost. When you reach the shoulder, it's time to initiate the blunt. Turn your body aggressively into your spin (upstream and downward) and plant your paddle deeply in the greenwater as a brake/pivot. When this stroke engages, push your stern into the air, throw your weight forward, and snap your boat onto its other edge. Make sure that you've pulled your bow to at least 12 o'clock before it enters the water; otherwise you'll catch your upstream edge and face plant.

Starting at the top of the wave, build as much speed as possible as you carve towards the shoulder. Here, a power stroke gives an added boost.

If you've built up good speed on your approach, then the success of your blunt will depend on your ability to release the stern from the water and throw it high into the air. This requires your movements to be quick and powerful. To get the most snap for this, you'll need to maximize your weight and edge transitions. To do this, shift your weight back and edge your boat aggressively into the wave, just before you engage your backstroke. This lifts your bow further off the water and is commonly referred to as 'loading the stern'. Now, when you plant your backstroke and initiate the blunt, you can make the largest and most powerful weight and edge transitions.

Though this whole procedure may sound difficult, if you look closely at the initiation of the blunt, you'll notice that we're really just talking about a highly aggressive bow pivot turn.

a) Reaching the shoulder at maximum speed, keep your boat carving, plant a back sweep at your hip, and turn your upper body to face the water.

b) Snap your weight forward and your boat onto its other edge while you push the stern into the air with your back sweep.

A successful blunt will land a paddler in a controlled back surf, and this recovery requires great edge control. When the blunt is initiated, your stern flies through the air with an incredible amount of spin momentum. As your stern passes vertical and falls downward, it will want to continue on its path and slice into the greenwater. To land in a back surf you'll need to flatten your boat before your stern hits the water. Your knees and hips are responsible for making this edge transition. You can also use a recovery stroke to regain control. The recovery stroke is a powerful backstroke that is taken just as your stern touches down. This stops your spin momentum and gives you

As the stern slices towards the water, level off your boat quickly to land in a back surf.

A powerful backstroke/ recovery stroke helps kill your spin momentum and keep you on the wave.

a good upstream push to keep you on the wave. It also provides you with a brace to regain your balance. This stroke is especially helpful on small waves, or if you've caught too much greenwater with your bow and are being pulled downstream.

Mastering the blunt is a major achievement and demonstrates that you have the skills and the power needed for ANY play move. But can you do it in reverse? Next up, the backstab.

Overview - Blunts

- Set-up: Start at the peak of the wave and, staying fairly high on the wave face, carve aggressively to the shoulder.
- Initiation: Push your stern into the air with an aggressive 'bow pivot turn'. Make sure your bow doesn't enter the water before being pulled to 12 o'clock.
- Recovery: Level off your kayak before the stern hits and follow up with a recovery stroke.

BACKSTAB

The backstab is simply a blunt done in reverse. This means you'll aggressively move from a back surf to front surf, throwing your bow almost vertically into the air. The backstab is definitely one of the trickiest moves to master and requires awesome back surfing control and awareness, as you'll need an aggressive set-up, initiation, and recovery.

The backstab is set up in the same way as the blunt, only you'll be doing it in a back surf. The key is building up speed and carving as aggressively as possible towards the wave's shoulder, without sliding too far down the wave's face. This means starting high up the face, pointing to the shoulder, and getting your boat on a carving edge. The backstab is initiated at the shoulder of the wave, when you've reached full speed. Initiating the backstab involves releasing your bow from the wave, and throwing it into the air. You'll do this with a snap, provided by a powerful edge and weight transition, along with what is basically a well-timed, ultra-aggressive stern pivot turn. The snap comes from having your weight forward and your boat carving hard on edge before your backstab is initiated. When the time comes to initiate the move, lead aggressively with your head and body, and plant a powerful forward sweep at your toes on the upstream side of your kayak. This stroke will pull your stern to 12 o'clock as you snap your boat onto its other edge and throw your weight slightly back.

Starting at the top of the wave, carve hard towards the shoulder, building as much speed as possible.

It is important that you don't lean right back when initiating the backstab, though it is tempting to do. If you want to get more snap from your weight transition, then lean further forward initially to 'load the bow'. When you pull on your sweep and make your edge transition, you can throw your weight back to a neutral position, where you'll have the most control over your edging. The timing of your stroke and your edge transition is also very important. Your stern needs to have been pulled all the way to 12 o'clock before it enters the greenwater. If you initiate your stern before having pulled it to 12 o'clock, you'll catch your upstream edge and find yourself face surfing before you know it. With a powerful snap and forward sweep, your bow should now be flying through the air.

Hit the shoulder at maximum speed and initiate the backstab with a powerful forward sweep, a snappy edge transition, and your head and body leading the way.

Notice that as the bow flies overhead, the body remains in a forward position. The power for the backstab comes largely from an aggressive edge transition and a powerful sweep stroke.

The final challenge is landing in a controlled front surf. The key to doing this is levelling off your kayak before your bow reaches the water. Your hips and knees are responsible for this edge transition, but a recovery stroke will also help out. This recovery stroke is a forward stroke taken on the opposite side from your initiation stroke, just before your bow touches down. This stroke does three things: it helps stop all your spin momentum, it provides a brace, and it provides forward power to keep you on the wave.

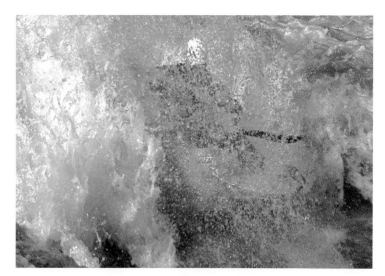

Unless you're planning on linking the backstab to another move, you'll want to stop and regain control in a frontsurf. The recovery stroke is a forward stroke that helps you do this.

I said at the beginning of this chapter that the backstab is one of the trickiest moves to master. The reason being that the set-up requires a high level of comfort and control while back surfing. Once you have this control, the backstab can be easier than the blunt because you're using the more powerful stern pivot turn instead of a bow pivot turn. With that said, the quickest way to start hitting this move is to develop your backward awareness and your back surfing, so keep working on all your backward skills!

Overview - Backstab

- Set-up: Start high on the wave in a back surf, carve aggressively to the shoulder, while not dropping too far down the wave.
- Initiation: At the shoulder of the wave and at full speed, throw your bow into the air with a snappy edge and weight transition, and an aggressive 'stern pivot turn'. Make sure your stern doesn't enter the water before it has reached 12 o'clock.
- Recovery: Before your bow touches down, level off your kayak and follow up with a powerful recovery stroke.

AERIALS

Clearly, lots of changes have taken place over the past 10 years, but in my opinion the most impressive developments have come from aerial moves. Aerial moves come into play in two ways. You can get air by diving your bow or stern underwater and popping up ender-style, or you can get air on waves by transferring your forward speed into upward lift. The pop-up technique lets you get air for moves like the loop or the space Godzilla. The transfer technique allows you to do aerial blunts, back stabs, Pan Ams, donkey flips, etc... Regardless of which method you're using, the shorter boats will always work the best.

Catching air for hole-based moves like the loop or the space Godzilla is a matter of timing, though having the right equipment will help a great deal. To get the most pop, you'll want a short boat with some decent volume. As you pop into the air, you can actually help get yourself airborne by jumping off your foot pegs. The key is timing your jump, and we take a detailed look at this in the 'Loop' segment.

Catching air on waves is much more technical and can be done in a couple of ways. You can carve your way into the air, bounce your way into the air, or use a combination of the two. For the most air, you'll use a combination of the two techniques, and Corran's segment about catching air talks in detail about how to do so. To establish a foundation though, we'll look at both of these techniques on their own.

Bouncing is definitely the easiest technique for getting air. It involves shooting down the face of a wave and alternately weighting your bow and stern by shifting your body weight in rhythm with the bounces that your boat naturally wants to make. In this way it is similar to the bobbing drill we looked at in the 'Getting Vertical' segment, except your boat stays flat, rather than on edge. Keep in mind that staying in rhythm means staying ahead of your kayak! This means that when your bow is down, your body should already be going back, and when your stern is down, you should already be leaning forward to get the bow back down.

Let's look at all this from the beginning. Start at the top of a wave, where it is the steepest. When you're at the top of a wave, your kayak will be balanced on the peak so that your bow is totally clear of the water. Point yourself directly upstream so you'll shoot down the face of the wave. As you begin sliding down the face, your bow will drop down to the wave. As your bow drops, encourage it down by leaning forward and pushing down with your feet and knees. Ideally, you'll press the bow into the wave as far as possible without having your bow dive right underwater. By encouraging it down like this, the bow will be rejected forcefully by the oncoming water, which initiates your bounce. Before your bow has had a chance to pop up, you should already be starting to lean back, and be pulling up with your knees to help your bow rise. If you time this right, your bow will pop quite aggressively out of the water. Now, as your bow reaches the peak of its pop, you should shifting your weight forward to press the bow down once again, and to pop the stern out of the water.

Depending on the situation, you'll get your best air from either your first or your second bounce. On really big waves, you'll often get highest from your second bounce. Regardless of which bounce you choose to use, you will initiate your move as your kayak reaches the top of its pop.

As you get better with the bouncing technique, you'll find yourself using it in a variety of situations. Though you may not get aerial with the bounce, it will let you momentarily un-weight your kayak so that you'll catch less greenwater when you initiate a move. This is why you see some of the best boaters doing mini-bounces on small waves to help their spins or blunts.

Carving, or the edge-transfer technique of catching air, is a more technical means of getting airborne, but it is very important to learn as it allows you to harness the most power with the widest range of boats. More importantly, the skills you'll need for this technique are the same, essential skills that so many other advanced playboating moves require. As a key innovator of aerial moves, Corran is the perfect person to explain how this actually happens and he does so in his upcoming segment.

UNDERSTANDING RELEASE AND AIR - BY CORRAN ADDISON

The same features that allow your kayak to spin, allow it to air. Release is the key. You need to release water from the hull, the edges and if necessary, the deck. As you progress through freestyle moves, the more important the individual and combined body movements, edge relations and water reading skills become. The same subtleties that made the difference between that clean 360 spin and a clean 540 spin, will make the difference between getting big air, or none at all.

You must first understand that there are several forces working on the hull of your kayak. Newton's 3rd law is as active here as anywhere: for every action there is an equal and opposite reaction. Your goal is to be free and clear before that opposite reaction becomes a burden on you.

With the current trend towards short, bouncy boats, basic aerial moves are becoming as simple as the flat spin. But beware... the techniques used to pop a small 'butt bouncer' off the water are not the same skills you'll need to be able to sky any boat. These butt bouncers offer you instant satisfaction, but the potential of such a style is finite. Unless you figure out the finer points of catching air, you'll never tap into the huge airs.

The biggest airs come from speed, the relation of that speed to the water, and how you transfer that forward moving energy into upward moving energy. Go back a few chapters to where Ken teaches you to blunt and notice his emphasis on speed and carving, angulation and edge transfer. Yes, a blunt "can" be performed in some boats by surfing near the top of a wave and forcing the nose to slice under your body, but this skill will work only some of the time, in some places, and have limited transfer to future moves. Before you embark on this chapter, make sure that you have truly learned how to speed away from your starting point, carving on a hard edge, and using dramatic and sudden edge transfers to release your edges. If you're still sitting flat in the 'butt surfer', go back and learn to carve.

THE AIR BLUNT – BY CORRAN ADDISON

The air blunt is the most simple and fundamental of aerial moves. You need to use the energy associated with the transfer of your weight from one carving edge to another, to get your kayak to forcibly explode into the air.

Starting from the top of the wave, where you'll get the greatest acceleration and final top speed, surf across the wave face with your boat on hard edge. Edging as you know comes from the legs and hips, and this is the part of the kayak that should be engaged, not from the hips back. The wide part of a good carving kayak is found in front of the hips. Use this wide point by getting on edge and consciously pressing it into the wave as you accelerate down its face. If your stern slides out, it's because your weight is too far back, or because you're not digging your front rail in enough. Though they are not a necessity, fins make it much easier to ride along the bow rail without stern slippage because they hold the tail in place.

For your first few tries, don't worry about getting airborne. Drop in, get the boat hard on edge, and feel the boat accelerate. As you accelerate, the nose is going to want to lift up. This is due to two things:

1. Most whitewater kayaks have stern rocker. The more rocker the kayak has, the faster the water travelling under the kayak has to accelerate to fill in the hole left by the kayak's depression. Water acceleration means a low-pressure zone, which translates into the sucking down of the stern into the low-pressure area.

2. The bow has its own wake. As you accelerate, the kayak is going to climb up this wake. This lifts the nose of the kayak upwards. The less efficient the planing surface, the sooner your kayak will want to climb its own wake.

The combination of these effects will cause your bow to lift and your stern to drop. The greater this movement, the less of a rail carve the bow will be able to execute. This will make it easier to "pop" the boat free of the water at low speeds, but will afford less opportunity for really big, spiraling aerials. Remember, top speed and the "G" forces from the turn are what give us the biggest airs. The sooner a boat hits its top carving speed, the less potential there is for great tricks. You can overcome this to a degree by maintaining that carving rail, and minimizing stern slip and stern sink as the kayak accelerates. Shifting your weight back only makes the problem worse, and I'm afraid that this is the default position of most paddlers.

Carving effectively involves pressing the front edge of your boat into the wave, not the stern edge.

With your weight forward, the kayak will continue to carve along this bow rail. The nose will grab more water than the stern, and the downstream movement of the current will begin to turn the boat. Ideally, you'd want to turn and face slightly downstream as you carve, so that you can use the river's current to your advantage. However, it is very rare that a river wave will have enough size and room to allow this, so most of the time you'll have to content yourself with somewhere between a 45 to 90 degree carve from the main current. The harder and deeper you can sink that carving bow rail, the more explosion you're going to get.

For the purposes of this demonstration, let's say we're carving to the surfer's right. Your right rail is sunk, the bow is turned almost towards the right shore (river left), and the tail is washing slightly as the bow continues to climb. When you feel that you have reached the apex of your turn, energy and speed (looking for the best total combination of the three), you then aggressively throw your body weight forward, sinking that edge and the whole nose into the oncoming current (without burying the tip of the kayak). This pumping of the kayak into the water will quickly and forcefully be rejected. How much it is rejected depends on how fast you were going, how deep the bow edge was pushed, and how many "G's" you have going in the carve. The greater that all these factors are, the greater the forces working against you, and the more forcefully your pressure on the bow is going to be rejected, and this you want!

As any woman will tell you, timing is everything. This is no less important for the air blunt, as the slightest miscalculation will result in little to no air, and loss of rotation along all axes. As your bow is acutely and decisively rejected, and your right carving rail is ejected from the water, the bow will rise. This movement you accentuate by aggressively throwing your weight back, with all energy still on the right rail. Again, timing is everything. As the bow reaches its peak, you need to once more aggressively throw your weight forward, but this time combine it with an edge transfer. Your goal is to bring the stern up to match the height of the bow… and indeed more. The more speed and carve you have, the higher the bow is going to be. As you throw your weight forward once more, you need to aggressively transfer all your weight from that right edge to your left edge, the same part located between your hips and your feet, and not the bow as you would suppose. This movement is helped by dropping your head in front and below your left shoulder, and also by keeping your eyes fixed on the pit of the wave below you. In addition, the paddle, which until now has been doing very little, becomes active. The left blade is dropped, in conjunction with your weight and edge transition, into a light stern pry (located at the hip, or slightly forward of the hip). The idea is to lift the stern over your body, not to slice the bow under your body. The combination of these movements sets you up for this, but you actually have to think it: stern up and over, not bow slicing under! The stern will arc

While carving aggressively, lean forward and press the bow rail into the wave.

As the bow gets rejected, help it bounce out of the water by throwing your weight back. As the bow reaches its apex, throw your weight forward and snap onto your other edge while pushing the stern over your body.

over, the bow will remain almost where it was, pointing down into the pit, and you'll land a boat-length upstream of where you took off, flat, in a back surf. Some waves require a back recovery stroke on landing to ensure you remain on the wave. This unfortunately ends all possibility of turning that air blunt into an air superblunt (which links clean spins on the exit of the air blunt) but it sure beats flushing.

Chad going airborne.

Overview - Air Blunt

- *Top speed and a hard carve are the number one contributors to big air.*
- *The amount of edge transfer you have is second in importance. The more edge to edge transfer, the bigger the air.*
- *Bounce, while significantly less important, is also necessary. Your radical weight transfers from bow to stern and back to bow are necessary.*
- *Timing all of the above to coincide with a natural boil or irregularity on the wave will accentuate your weight transfers and give you bigger air.*
- *Avoid multiple bounces. Each bounce is significantly smaller than the one before. Your first pop from a hard fast carve is your best chance at huge air.*

PAN AM - BY CORRAN ADDISON

Aah… the infamous Pan Am. Soon after I realized that the key to big blunts was not bounce, but speed, carve and edge transfer, I began to wonder how far I could take that edge transfer. I asked myself, "Is it possible to do a full pirouette while vertical and airborne". The answer I discovered was YES! However, it took several weeks of falling on my head to come to this conclusion. In fact it was named a Pan Am because I would take off, and then instantly go into a spiraling twisting dive and crash. So, do not be dissuaded if it doesn't come to you instantly.

If you're into simply bouncing your way to air blunts, you can skip this chapter. You will NEVER do a Pan Am like this. The body position and boat position of a bounced air blunt is simply at odds with the rotations and height needed to pull this off. A carved air blunt is required to do this. For practicality's sake, our demonstration here will also be to the right.

The Pan Am takes off on its right edge, and lands once more on the right edge. If you land with your hull facing upstream, or on your left edge, all you get is one BIG air blunt. The set-up and requirements for a Pan Am are the same as for an air blunt. I found the effects of fins here to be highly advantageous, but I know it can be done without. Fins allow you to get the most energy transfer from the ejection of the bow, into the spiral. Like setting up the air blunt, you'll race at 45 degrees or more across the face of a wave, the right edge of the kayak from your feet to your hips engaged deeply. When your edge is loaded with maximum energy, you've reached the crucial moment, and you must have total confidence that you have enough energy built up to complete the move.

At maximum speed, and with the carving edge loaded, pop the bow into the air by weighting, then unweighting the bow.

The beginning movements are the same as the air blunt. You weight the bow to sink the right edge as deeply as you can, without it diving underwater. You then throw your weight back as the bow is rejected to get maximum height from your bow. Now, rather than weighting the bow again, while simultaneously dropping your head and looking into the pit, you change tactics. The left paddle is planted a little earlier, which enables you to accentuate and begin earlier the transfer from the right to left edge. As the left blade engages the water, and the bow reaches its apex with the right edge still engaged, you throw your weight forward once more and at the same time, rotate your head to look up and over your left shoulder just as you would doing a backstroke pirouette out of a hole. As the bow drops, and the stern lifts over the bow, the kayak pirouettes in the air. It is key to keep looking over your left shoulder and not at the pit of the wave, and to take the left blade out of the water as soon as the stroke is done. After the kayak passes over top the body, the right edge of the kayak will slice into the face of the wave. If you still have good rotation, your stern will slice into the wave, and you'll end up in a front surf.

While pushing off the backstroke and snapping the boat onto the other edge, turn the head aggressively to look over the shoulder and lead the pirouette.

A number of things can happen throughout the move, but as long as the first edge to contact the water is your right edge, and not the left or the hull, it's a Pan Am. In a rodeo, you'll need to come to flat at the end to complete the move, but in free-surfing, landing on your right edge is all you need to pat yourself on the back.

As the boat lands on edge, the stern slices through, resulting in a front surf.

Overview - Pan Am

- Top speed and the precision of the carve is key.
- The pop from the carve, combined with radical rotation is needed to take the kayak beyond a normal air blunt.
- Do not look at the pit of the wave, but rather over your shoulder as in a pirouette.
- The first edge to engage the water must be the same edge that left the water.

Air Screw / Donkey Flip -
by Corran Addison

photos by Rob Faubert

The air screw is the natural progression of the Pan Am. The primary difference between a Pan Am and an air screw is that for the air screw the nose of the kayak never drops under the stern. The kayak remains horizontal during the majority of the 360 degree rotation.

The set-up is much like the Pan Am, but this is in fact one of the moves which can be done by bouncing the boat into the air, rather than using a carving approach. However, because I am convinced that in almost every other situation a carving approach is best, I'm going to teach you this move in the same way.

Once more, we will perform this demonstration while carving to the right. I go through the same motions as I did for the Pan Am, except that my point of take-off is facing directly upstream rather than between 45 and 90 degrees to the main current. In order to reach maximum carve and speed while facing directly upstream, I won't start pointing upstream. I begin from the right side of the wave and carve left at between 45 to 90 degrees. As I approach the centre of the wave, I drop my right edge in, and engage it from my feet to my hips. This turns the kayak to face directly upstream as I accelerate to full speed. This way, I am able to accelerate and carve into the move, rather than simply facing upstream and bouncing the kayak into the air, which as I have already stressed, will give you far less air, and certainly less rotation.

As before, when it's time for take-off, I press the right edge of the kayak into the wave and generate as much pressure under it as I can. As the edge is rejected, I throw my weight back as before and get my nose as high as possible. This time, while throwing my weight back, I also begin my rotation over the left edge, with my head looking back over my left shoulder. Your kayak will follow your head, so make sure you look as far up and back as you can. At this same time, the left blade can push off the water to provide added leverage for the boat rotation. As this left stern pry makes its push, the right hand should arch up and over your head, following your gaze up and over your left shoulder. Don't be afraid to lift your right elbow high into the air. Too much left pry will pull your bow down so don't rely on your paddle. In fact, I have come to realize that doing this move cleanly is ideal for success since the bow remains pointing skyward.

As the bow reaches its peak, the body is thrown back and turned into the spin. In this case, Billy is pushing lightly off the power face of his left blade while his right arm punches over his head, without being overextended.

Once past half-way, the right blade can skim the surface to help complete the rotation.

As you become inverted, with the kayak completely upside down and the bow still elevated, it is important to keep your head and eyes rotating. At this same time, your right paddle blade will sweep over the surface of the water. Every effort should be made for this not to contact the water until it is past half-way, as this will also kill your rotation. Once past half-way you can let the face or back of the blade, according to your preference, skim across the surface helping to complete the rotation and push you back up.

Two vital factors are needed for the air screw to be an air screw, and not some other fumbled rendition of an undefined move. The first is that the boat should remain relatively horizontal for the majority of the move. I say relatively, because short of getting 6 feet of air, a feat I have accomplished only a few times, the nose will invariably drop. My second stipulation is that you land on the same edge from which you took off. In the case we've considered, take-off was on the right edge, so the kayak must land on the right edge, or better, flat on the hull.

Clearly, the air screw is most spectacular when done cleanly, but of course, edge timing becomes paramount. So, begin as I have described here, and then as you become more comfortable, start to do the rotation purely by leading with your head and not pushing off the paddle. When you lead aggressively with your head, good things will happen.

To finish the move, the body stays on the back deck, the right blade sculls the surface, and the head continues to lead the way.

Overview - Air Screw / Donkey Flip

- *A combination of speed, a hard carve, and bounce is the most effective way of setting up this move.*
- *The rotation begins as the bow lifts into the air, and not as the stern climbs as with the Pan Am.*
- *Look aggressively up and over your shoulder to lead the move.*
- *You must land on the same edge from which you took off, or flat on the hull, for the move to be complete.*

THE AERIAL FLIP TURN -
BY STEVE FISHER

photos by Dan Campbell

The aerial flip turn is one of my favourite moves, as well as one of the most dynamic and aggressive moves that I know. You will need a fairly large, fast wave and a high performance kayak - one with a hard carving edge and/or fins. The edges of fins ensure that the kayak grabs as much water as possible whilst carving, so that when the edge is released, it is ready to explode out of the water. The goal of the move is to over-edge your boat while carving or turning, so that the boat shoots into the air as a result of the force between the hull and the fast moving greenwater.

Step one:

Start in a neutral position as close to the top of the wave as possible. Let your boat surge down the face of the wave and gain speed. When you reach your maximum speed, use a stern pry to start turning your kayak, giving it spin momentum. Bouncing the boat slightly can help at this point.

Step two:

When your boat is almost sideways use an aggressive 'hip flick' to over-edge your boat (tilting it very hard downstream). As you do this, the oncoming water hits the flat hull of your kayak and wants to push your boat downstream, but because of all your forward speed, the only direction the greenwater can push you is upward. Now lift your paddle out of the water and enjoy the 'take off'.

Step three:

At this point if you do nothing you will crash and burn: either you will land upside down, or your bow will hit the water and take you out. By planting a forward sweep/brace on the downstream side, your bow will be pushed up and your stern will hit the water first. The more air you get from the take-off and the later you plant your sweep, the more your stern will be allowed to rotate around and the more radical the move will be. (This is the turning point between a flip turn and a helix.)

As you reach maximum speed, get the boat turning sideways then aggressively over-edge the boat downstream. The oncoming water will help pop your boat into the air, and over top your body.

Plant a sweep stroke on the downstream side to pull your stern down, then kick your legs forward and lean back to re-establish your front surf.

Step four:

Your stern hits the water, and you help the bow settle back down by thrusting your legs forward and lying your body on your back deck. This move catches a lot of water, and can easily pull you off the wave, so sit upright and take some forward strokes as soon as you can.

Like many of the high end wave moves, the flip turn will require every ounce of your strength and total commitment. Believe it or not, it is not as technically difficult as you might think, but I guarantee you that you'll have an aching body after a day of flip turns.

Overview - Flip Turn

- Start at the top of the wave, and let your boat drop down the wave, gathering as much speed as possible.
- When you reach maximum speed, use a stern pry to get your boat turning sideways then aggressively snap your hips and over-edge the boat downstream.
- Keep your paddle out of the water and let the boat pop into the air, over top your body.
- When it's time to regain control, plant a forward sweep on the downstream side and pull your stern to the water while kicking your legs out.

THE HELIX - BY STEVE FISHER

The Zambezi River has to be the best playboating river in the world. It's got everything you'd want, from mammoth standing waves to perfect holes. The big play waves have been the perfect place for me to learn, discover, and invent new playboating moves. Here's the latest trick that I've invented, the helix.

The helix is basically an upside-down 360. If you can do a good, radical aerial flip turn then you can probably do a helix, because it is just an extension of that move. To do either the flip turn or the helix, you'll need a high performance boat, a big, fast wave and a lot of commitment.

Looking back to the flip turn, you started at the top of a wave, then shot down its face, gathering as much speed as possible. When you reached your maximum speed, you started your boat spinning with a back sweep. When your boat reached sideways to the main current, you used a powerful 'hip flick' to over-edge your boat downstream. This bounced your kayak right into the air while your body stayed tucked forward at water level. Before your boat fell back to the water, you then planted a forward sweep/brace on the downstream side and kicked your legs out, which pushed your bow into the air, and pulled your stern down to hit the water. This is the turning point between a flip turn and a helix. Instead of planting your sweep and kicking your legs out, stay tucked forward, let your stern continue to rotate around, and reach for a stroke with your other paddle blade. This aggressive switch to the other blade and the twist of your body causes the boat to continue rotating above you on a horizontal plane. As the boat comes around on a full 360-degree rotation, roll the boat back upright and kick your legs out to land in a front surf.

Overview - Helix

- *Initiate as an aggressive flip turn: speed, bounce, and a powerful hip flick.*
- *Stay tucked forward and let the stern rotate upstream.*
- *As the stern reaches 12 o'clock, reach for the greenwater with your other paddle blade.*
- *As the boat comes around, roll up and kick your legs out to land in a front surf.*

photos by Dale Jardine

Hole Moves

SIDE SURFING

Side surfing is the act of balancing in the trough of a hole, using the hole's re-circulating water to keep you in place. If you're just learning to side surf, then you may have trouble believing that side surfing is a passive skill that relies completely on balance. But trust me on this one! Even the biggest, juiciest holes can be relatively easy to surf. It's getting out that causes the most problems! The reality is that side surfing is one of the most intimidating skills to learn, but it can be lots of fun, and is an essential playboating skill to master if you want to take your paddling to the next level.

Brendan Mark in a BIG hole

The Balancing Act

Staying upright in a side surf requires lifting your upstream edge so that it won't catch the water pouring into the hole. If this upstream edge does catch, you're looking at a super quick flip, better known as the 'Wathunk'. Holding this downstream tilt is a balancing act, but you already have the skills. Shift your weight onto your downstream butt cheek, pull upwards on the thigh brace with your upstream knee/thigh and push down and outwards with your downstream knee/thigh. Since most flips are caused by the stern edges of the kayak getting caught, stay in an aggressive position to lift those stern edges. You should also always be looking upstream. It doesn't matter if your kayak is facing upstream, downstream or sideways, keep your eyes on the trough of the hole. So how much downstream tilt do you need while side surfing? Ideally your kayak should be on edge enough to prevent your upstream edge from catching, but no more. Any extra tilt will make balancing more difficult and will result in a rougher ride as more water hits the hull of your kayak. It should be clear at this point that side surfing doesn't involve leaning on your paddle. Side surfing is simply a balancing act. So what does the paddle do? The paddle has two responsibilities: you'll use it as a brace, and you'll use it to move around.

Side surfing is a balancing act. With your weight balanced on the downstream hip/butt cheek, your paddle is free to take strokes. Notice the boat is tilted only enough to keep the upstream edge from catching, no more.

Bracing: If you're not actively stroking, your paddle should be ready as a brace. With that said, it is important to understand that a brace is very different from a crutch. A crutch gets leaned on, whereas a brace is used to temporarily stop yourself from flipping when you've lost your balance. The type of brace you use will depend on your situation, but whether you're using a high brace or a low brace, make sure you keep your paddle below your chin and don't overextend your arms. When you start overreaching with your brace, your shoulders are at risk. If for some reason you happen to catch your upstream edge, nothing is going to save you, so tuck up and prepare to roll on the downstream side. In this situation experienced freestyle paddlers use the back deck roll! Whatever you do, do NOT try to brace on the

While being bounced around in a hole, the low brace is held close to the body, ready for action.

upstream side! You won't save yourself, and will probably slam your paddle into rocks, which often results in a broken paddle, a damaged ego, and sometimes even a dislocated shoulder.

Strokes: First and foremost, all your strokes need to be taken on the downstream side of your kayak. If you take a stroke on the upstream side, you'll be blowing bubbles before you know it! These strokes should reach under the foam pile and grab the greenwater that is flowing under the hull of your kayak, because the aerated foam pile doesn't provide enough substance for an efficient stroke. You'll know when you've reached the greenwater, as it feels very solid. By doing this, you can take powerful forward and backward strokes and use stationary strokes. A stationary stroke is a stroke that actively applies pressure to move your kayak without your paddle changing position relative to your boat and body. You can take both forward and backward stationary strokes. In the case of the braking/backward stationary stroke, by planting your paddle deeply in the greenwater and curling your wrists slightly downward, water will hit the backside of your paddle blade, which can be pushed upon to achieve a continuous, powerful backstroke. Similarly, you can use a stationary forward stroke to move yourself forward in a hole. In this case, your paddle gets planted with your wrists cocked slightly back so that the power face of your blade is catching water. You can now pull on your paddle and apply steady pressure to achieve a continuous forward stroke. These stationary strokes are very powerful ways of moving around in a hole.

All strokes should be taken on the downstream side and planted deep enough to grab the greenwater below the foam pile.

- Balance your weight on your downstream butt cheek and hold a steady tilt by pulling up with your upstream knee and pushing down with your downstream knee.
- Keep your weight on your butt and off your paddle.
- Tilt the kayak JUST enough to prevent the upstream edge from catching. Any extra tilt will make balancing more difficult.
- Have your paddle READY in a low or low-high brace position on the downstream side. Never brace or take strokes on the upstream side.
- Plant your strokes in the greenwater under the foam pile.

Entering the Hole

Now that you know what to do in a hole, let's take a look at the best ways of getting in there to begin with. There are two good ways of establishing a sidesurf: you can slide in, or you can drop in.

Sliding in from an abutting eddy is easiest because there is no downstream momentum to control. You'll have to be careful that you don't enter too far upstream where the main current can catch your bow. Look to turn, or ferry into a hole, with your bow staying near the trough, and your body just upstream of the boil line. As you turn into the hole, keep your weight over the kayak and on your downstream butt cheek while your knees pull and push on the thigh braces to help keep a steady downstream boat tilt. Your paddle should be ready in a low brace, or a low-high brace position on the downstream side in case you lose your balance. Do NOT take any strokes on the upstream side of your kayak, as the water will grab your paddle blade and throw you upside down in a flash. Now as you slide into the hole sideways, your low brace can act as a brake to stop you from shooting out the far side of the hole. As we already discussed, the braking stroke involves reaching down to the greenwater with your wrists curled slightly forward so that the current is hitting the backside of your paddle.

Slide into the trough of the hole with a low brace at the ready. This low brace becomes a braking stroke that stops you in the hole.

Dropping into a hole can be a bit trickier as the foam pile stops your kayak while your body wants to continue downstream. Let's look at how to compensate for this sudden change. First off, you're going to have to convince yourself that you really WANT to be in that hole. Floating sideways, line up to hit a part of the hole that is powerful enough to stop your downstream momentum. When the main current is fast, you can expect a good hit from the foam pile. Stay loose in the hips and anticipate the amount of brace that you'll need to stay upright. As you hit the foam pile, commit to this low brace on the down-stream side, as there's no point trying to stay balanced over your kayak. The sudden change in momentum just won't let you. The key is now understanding that the brace isn't there to lean on. It's there to stop you from falling face first into the foam pile and to provide a platform from which you can immediately push your weight back up and over your kayak. As a final note, be sure to keep your weight forward the whole time so that your stern edges don't get caught by the oncoming water. Sometimes, a hole will surge or won't be strong enough to stop your momentum. If you don't think the hole is powerful enough to completely stop you, point yourself upstream and slow yourself down with some forward strokes. When you feel the hole hit you in the back, let your kayak slide into a side surf (not carve) by throwing your weight forward and pushing off a back sweep on the downstream side. This will be easiest if you aren't pointing directly upstream as you can fall into the surf on a predetermined side.

When dropping into a hole, brace into it upon impact, but get your weight back over your kayak as quickly as possible. Note the body stays forward at all times.

Escaping the Hole's Grasp

Getting into a hole isn't so tough. Settling into a balanced side surf isn't so hard either. But boy, can getting out of a hole ever be a pain in the butt! You first need to understand that the only reliable places to get out of a hole are at the corners, or at a weak spot such as a tongue. The key to getting out is staying relaxed and keeping your weight over your kayak. When panic sets in, paddlers tend to start using their paddles as crutches. Once this happens, the chances of escaping in control drop considerably. Relax! Often a powerful stationary stroke will take you right out the side of a sticky hole. In stickier holes, you may need to work your way back and forth to the corners of the hole to build the speed necessary to punch out the side.

When you really want to get out of a hole though, blasting is usually your best bet. This means front surfing a hole. It is quite easy to get a playboat into the blasting position, but it is much more difficult to hold your boat like this. To establish a blast, take a powerful sweep stroke on the downstream side with your kayak kept as flat to the surface of the water as possible. Now if you're trying to get out of the hole, don't bring your boat right up to 12 o'clock! Stop at a ferry angle, then tilt your boat slightly on edge to get your boat carving. Instead of skidding back into a side surf, your kayak will carve hard and quickly out the side of the hole. Freedom!

Pulling the boat into a ferry/blast, then carving out the side is one of the most powerful and effective ways of escaping a hole.

360's

360's provide the foundation for many of the advanced moves and they are the ultimate test of your ability to work with, and not against, the power of the river. You need to have a good awareness of your position in a hole and quick and stable weight and edging transitions. Thanks to the flat hulls and slicey ends of today's kayaks, flat-spinning techniques can also be incorporated to make your spins quicker and more controlled. But let's start by looking at the most basic 360.

360's are easiest when a hole has a spin corner to work with. A spin corner is a corner that feeds water (and paddlers) back into the hole. To do a 360, you'll need to stay balanced over your kayak, leaving your paddle free to move you around the hole. As discussed in the 'Side Surfing' segment, this means keeping your weight on your downstream butt cheek. Looking over your upstream shoulder, work your way to the corner of the hole and let your bow get taken downstream until your kayak is parallel to the main current. Without pulling yourself right out, you need to reach a point far enough out of the hole where your stern won't catch when you switch edges. As each hole is different, it may take a few tries to find this point, so approach the corner slowly to begin with. If you feel yourself being drawn back into the hole and aren't sure that you can complete the spin, don't fight the water. Keep your boat on edge and let yourself slide back in, then try again. Eventually, with your weight forward,

Keep your eyes upstream and your weight forward as you try to reach a point far enough out of the hole where your stern won't catch.

you will reach a point where your stern is clear of the greenwater and your bow points to 6 o'clock. Now keep the spin going by planting a forward sweep/high brace on the other side, looking upstream over your other shoulder, and tilting your kayak in the other direction by shifting your weight from one butt cheek to the other. In general you won't need very aggressive boat tilts. Not only is it harder to balance when your boat is right up on edge, but you can end up carving yourself right out of a hole. On the other hand, if your boat is too flat, your stern can easily catch the greenwater.

When your bow reaches 6 o'clock, keep the spin going by planting your next stroke, looking over the other shoulder and tilting your boat on its other edge.

The second half of the 360 tends to be easier since your back won't ever be turned to the hole. This time, back paddle to reach that same balance point up on the corner of the hole. Once there, plant a brake/low brace on the other side, and swap boat tilts while leaning back slightly to keep your bow from diving.

Finishing the 360. Note the braking stroke that helps turn the kayak while preventing the bow from catching green-water.

Overview - 360's

- *Spin at the corners or tongues of a hole, letting the water do as much of the work as possible.*
- *Keep your weight over the kayak and off the paddle as much as possible.*
- *Keeping your eyes over your upstream shoulder and your weight forward, paddle up the corner until your kayak points to 6 o'clock and your stern is clear of the greenwater. Then switch strokes and boat tilts, look upstream over the opposite shoulder, and let yourself slide back into the hole.*
- *Don't force the 360. If you don't reach 6 o'clock, let yourself slide back in, then try again.*

The 360 isn't an easy move to master because you need to be comfortable being backwards in a hole. Reaching this comfort level will take plenty of practice. This is just another great reason to work on your back eddy turns, ferries and surfing. The more comfortable you are with being backward, the easier the 360, or any other advanced move will be.

Elevated 360's

The elevated 360 represents your first major step into the world of verticality and is a very simple adaptation of the 360 we just covered. The idea behind the elevated 360 is to pull your stern underwater for the second half of the spin. By pulling your stern underwater, a portion of your 360 acts as a pivot turn. As we saw in the 'Pivot Turns' segment, this is a very aggressive turn and skill linked closely to the more advanced vertical moves such as cartwheels.

Let's look at this from the beginning of the basic 360. From a side surf, work your way to the spin corner and with your eyes kept upstream, let your bow get taken downstream. As your kayak passes 6 o'clock, roll your boat onto its other edge, look upstream over your other shoulder and plant a forward sweep stroke on the downstream side of your kayak. We're now jumping right back to the stern pivot turn we covered earlier: With your head and body leading the way, and your boat tilted slightly into your sweep, you can pull your stern

underwater and lift your bow into the air. When doing this in a hole, you'll be sinking your stern into the fast moving water below the foam pile, which will give your pivot turn an added boost. As with the pivot turn on flatwater, the key is to level off your boat tilt before your sweep stroke has finished. This prevents your kayak from hitting the wall. With a powerful sweep and good edge transitions, your bow should swing powerfully upstream. Don't forget to finish your pivot turn with your body weight forward, and don't let the kayak get ahead of you. Keep leading with your head and body at all times.

When you've passed 6 o'clock, the elevated 360 gets initiated as your basic stern pivot turn.

When you are comfortable with the stern pivot turn in a hole, you can start linking it to a bow pivot turn. To link a stern pivot turn to a bow pivot turn, change your tilt so that your bow slices downwards after your forward sweep has finished. As your spin momentum takes your bow downward, initiate your bow pivot turn: lead with the head and body, push your stern into the air with a back sweep and throw your weight forward to help force the bow down. This combination of stern to bow pivot turns is nothing short of an actual cartwheel! And so opens a whole new world of moves to you…

Pull the stern down aggressively, but level off your kayak before your stroke finishes.

Throughout the move, the body stays forward and the head leads the way.

Overview - Elevated 360's

- *Set-up as you would a standard 360.*
- *When your bow passes 6 o'clock, initiate a standard stern pivot turn.*
- *Level off your kayak before your sweep finishes to avoid hitting the wall.*
- *Finish with your body in an aggressive forward position.*

CARTWHEELS

Though it was once considered the ultimate playboating move, the cartwheel is now more of an essential playboating skill, as it provides the foundation for so many of the more advanced moves.

Like the flatwater cartwheel, the standard cartwheel is basically a smooth combination of bow and stern pivot turns, which results in the boat revolving around at a fairly consistent rate, with minimal lateral or vertical movement. Having to deal with the dynamics of a hole puts an interesting twist on things, since every hole you'll come across is different. Because of these differences, there is no one method of cartwheeling, but there are some standard techniques that can be slightly modified to fit any situation. These are the techniques that we're going to look at.

There are 3 components to the cartwheel: the set-up, the initiation, and the linking of ends.

The Set-up

A good set-up is vital for the success of any cartwheel. The goal

is to initiate the cartwheel at the seam of a hole, with as little upstream speed as possible and with some spin momentum already established. The only reliable way to do all this is by getting on top of the foam pile where you have the most control. For this reason, the cartwheel is often easiest to set up as you enter a hole. So instead of sliding into a side surf, ferry right onto the foam pile. If you're already side surfing in the trough of a hole, you'll need to work your way to a corner in order to get on top of the foam pile. One of the best ways of doing this is by blasting out to the side of the hole, then cutting back onto the foam pile. Once you're there, you'll find that staying on top of the foam pile isn't an easy thing to do, as the hole's re-circulating water wants to pull you back upstream. This is where braking strokes come in. These are the same braking strokes that we talked about in the aggressive front surfing chapter. Braking strokes are powerful backstrokes that get planted deeply at the hip and catch lots of greenwater. Using alternating braking strokes, you can stop yourself from being sucked into the trough of most moderately sized holes. These braking strokes also help you to set up the right initiation angle on your kayak, which brings us to the next step.

Once on top of the foam pile, braking strokes will control the speed at which you get pulled back into the hole, as well as the angle of your kayak.

Overview - Cartwheel Set-up

- *Establish control on the hole's foam pile.*
- *Use alternating braking strokes to slow, or stop yourself from being pulled back into the hole.*

The Set-up

There are 3 crucial rules for the initiation of the cartwheel.

#1 Initiate with as little upstream momentum as possible

The reason you want to initiate with as little upstream momentum as possible is because extra upstream momentum simply drives your kayak deeper into the greenwater. This will cause you to pop into the air 'ender-style', while the greenwater pushes you downstream, away from the hole. Neither of these results will help your cartwheel.

#2 Initiate your bow at the seam of the hole.

The cartwheel uses a combination of the river's power and your own power. Initiating at the seam of a hole tends to make for an even balance of the two.

#3 Initiate with spin momentum

Initiating with spin momentum means that you should already be pulling your bow around and downwards **before** it enters the water, instead of just relying on the current to take your bow downstream. You'll build this spin momentum by first establishing a set-up angle with braking strokes, then winding up your body, planting a back/braking stroke and pulling your bow around with your knees and stomach muscles (recognize the bow pivot turn?) If you need additional spin momentum, you can also use a small double pump to wind-up your bow.

As a general rule, we can say that if you intend to initiate a cartwheel to the left, you should set up with a slight angle to the right, and vice-versa. You've got two choices when deciding how to set up and initiate your cartwheel. Let's continue to consider a cartwheel to the left. By setting up at 1 o'clock and initiating your bow around 12 o'clock, you can expect to do vertical ends. In this case, your kayak should be tilted aggressively on edge with your spin momentum directed more vertically than laterally. Your other option is a low-angle cartwheel, where you set up somewhere around 1 o'clock and initiate between 12 and 11 o'clock. In this case, your kayak is tilted between 20 and 45 degrees, with more lateral spin momentum established. This cartwheel will act more like an elevated flat spin.

Now that you understand where and how to initiate, let's take a closer look at the techniques that will help you get the job done. First of all, let's look at the paddle.

A cartwheel to the left requires setting up with a slight angle to the right. The bow is initiated at the seam of the hole, having being pulled from 1 o'clock to 12 o'clock, and tilted on a steep edge. This initiation will provide fairly vertical cartwheels.

The paddle is responsible for three things: providing the braking power that will stop your kayak from diving too deeply into the green water, providing a pivot from which you can pull your kayak around using your knees and stomach muscles, and being available as a brace, though it isn't a crutch to lean on as your weight should stay over your kayak.

To do these things, the active blade reaches down at the hip to the greenwater under the foam pile, where your back/brake stroke will get the most power. Meanwhile, the top hand is held firmly in front of the body at shoulder level, about a foot in front of the chest. This top hand should never cross your chest! Once again we're looking at keeping a rectangle formed by your arms, paddle and chest, in a relatively fixed position. This is the 'power position', and is responsible for giving you the most power and for keeping your shoulders safe.

As for the rest of your body, you'll want to throw your weight forward to help initiate your bow. You'll also want to keep your eyes on the seam of the hole as you pull your bow downwards. This lets you keep track of your position in the hole and spot the landing for your stern. Keeping in mind that you need to stay ahead of your kayak's progression, the length of time you keep your eyes on the seam is dependent on the power of the hole and speed of your cartwheels. If you're initiating a cartwheel in a slow pour-over, you can keep looking upstream right up until your initiation stroke has finished, whereas in a powerful/fast hole, you're better off turning and leading the way with your head immediately after your bow has been initiated.

The initiation stroke is planted deeply at the hip. Note how aggressively the upper body is leading the way, while the paddle stays relatively fixed in the 'power position'.

If the hole isn't overly fast or powerful, keep your eyes on the seam of the hole (where you'll be initiating your stern next) until your initiation stroke reaches completion.

Initiating the stern of your kayak is slightly more difficult, only because you'll have to set up with your back to the hole. Once you're set-up though, you'll initiate the stern with the standard stern pivot turn that we covered in the 'Fundamental Skills' chapter. This means leading the way with your head and body as you take a powerful sweep stroke with your kayak tilted into the sweep. Don't count on the river to do the work for you. Pull aggressively on your sweep and force your stern underwater. Once you've pulled it under, be ready to level off your boat tilt before your stroke has finished, to avoid hitting the wall.

Overview - Initiation

- *Remember the 3 rules: 1. Initiate with as little upstream momentum as possible. 2. Initiate your bow at the seam of the hole. 3. Initiate with spin momentum*
- *If you intend to initiate to the left, set up with a slight angle to the right, and vice-versa.*
- *For the low-angle cartwheel: cut from 1 o'clock to between 12 and 11 o'clock, focus on lateral spin momentum and initiate your bow on between a 20-45 degree angle.*
- *For more vertical cartwheels: cut from 1 o'clock to 12 o'clock, focus on vertical spin momentum and tilt your boat aggressively on edge.*
- *Don't try to throw completely vertical cartwheels, as balance is extremely difficult. Shoot for 60-80 degrees.*

Linking Ends

Once you've initiated your bow, linking ends involves making smooth edge transitions, keeping your weight forward as much as possible, and moving quickly from one stroke to the next. Let's continue looking individually at the actions of your boat, body and paddle during a cartwheel initiated to the left.

Your boat: As with the flatwater cartwheel, before your initiation stroke has finished, you must have made your edge transition. If you haven't done so, you'll hit the wall, and your cartwheel will stall out or will get turned downstream in a pirouette. This is nothing new. It goes right back to the bow pivot turn we explored in the 'Fundamental Skills' segment. Of course, for the cartwheel you don't want to just level off your kayak. You want to tilt your kayak in the other direction. The amount you tilt your kayak depends on how vertical you want your cartwheel to be. A near-vertical cartwheel will require getting your kayak right on its other edge, whereas a low-angle cartwheel will require a less aggressive edge transition.

Your paddle: As you make your edge transition, you need to plant your next stroke as quickly as possible. It is here that the standard cartwheel differs from the flatwater cartwheel. On flatwater there is no current to help the cartwheel, so we reach all the way to our toes to get a powerful second stroke. When cartwheeling in a hole, it becomes more important to get your next stroke in the water as quickly as possible. This means that instead of taking the extra time to reach all the way to your toes for your second stroke, just drop your paddle into the greenwater somewhere between your hip and knee. You won't get as much pull from this stroke, but if you made

When one stroke is done, get the next stroke in the water right away. Notice that for this 2nd stroke, the paddle drops into the water between the hip and knee, and does not reach all the way to the toes.

smooth edge transitions, your kayak should be carrying plenty of spin momentum already and the water will be helping to push your boat around. With your next stroke in the water, you can continue to pull your bow around with your stomach and knees, while making any corrections before your boat has had the chance to travel off course. This applies to all your subsequent strokes as well. Don't bother reaching for any big strokes if you don't need to. Just drop your next blade into the water as quickly as possible, so that you can maintain control of your boat and continue to pull it around with your knees and stomach.

Your Body: When cartwheeling, there's no one position for your body. You'll constantly need to make adjustments. In general though, it's difficult to be leaning too far forward, while it is quite common to be leaning too far back. To break it down further, when your bow is down, your body is best in a neutral position, with some of your weight on your footpegs. When your stern is down, your weight should be in an aggressive, forward position. Though these body leans will play a major role in the success of your cartwheel, the most important job for your upper body is staying wound up and leading your kayak through each end. With your body wound up, your stomach and knees can continue to pull the bow around, while making small corrections along the way.

After the bow has been initiated, the body is usually best off in a relatively neutral position, with some weight on the footpegs.

With the stern initiated, your body should be in a moderately aggressive, forward position, and your head leads the way.

It's also important to consider where your eyes are during the cartwheel. Ideally your eyes will stay on the seam of the hole as much as possible. This way you can 'spot your landing' for every end. In slow-moving holes, or pour-overs, this is reasonable as you can look at the seam of the hole until your first stroke has finished. When you drop your next blade into the water, your head turns to look at the seam over the leading shoulder. These are usually the most controlled cartwheels. When holes become more powerful, cartwheels often happen too fast to be able to keep your eyes upstream for long. As the cartwheels speed up, you'll have to lead with your head earlier and earlier.

Cartwheeling is one of the most difficult freestyle moves to master for a reason. It involves the combination of all fundamental playboating skills, great balance and a keen awareness of how the current will affect your kayak. All these skills will take time to develop, but you can help them along by watching and learning from the best paddlers on the river.

1. Ideally, the eyes stay fixed on the seam of the hole until the first stroke has finished its job.

2. When the second stroke is dropped into the water, the head turns and looks over the other shoulder.

Overview - Linking Ends

- Make smooth edge transitions to maintain spin momentum and to avoid 'hitting the wall'.
- Use quick strokes. Don't take the time to reach for each stroke; just drop your next blade in the water to maintain power and control.
- Stay forward as much as possible and lead the cartwheel with your upper body.
- Keep your eyes on the seam of the hole as much as possible.

SPLITWHEELS

The splitwheel is an advanced move that involves changing the direction of a cartwheel sequence without pause. With that said, it should be obvious that in order to splitwheel you first need to be a confident cartwheeler. Assuming that you are, let's look at how the splitwheel works by comparing it to the basic cartwheel.

The cartwheel is initiated with your boat on edge, and your weight balanced on a single hip. By the time your initiation stroke has finished, you need to have shifted your weight onto your other hip. You then reach for your next stroke, and turn your head to lead the way. The splitwheel differs from the cartwheel in that you don't make any of these transitions. You'll actually keep your weight over the same edge, keep the same blade in the water, and look over the same shoulder throughout the move.

Let's look at the move from the beginning, with a cartwheel initiated to the paddler's right. Keep in mind that you don't want to initiate a vertical cartwheel for the splitwheel. A vertical cartwheel will make balancing MUCH more difficult. Look to throw each end of the splitwheel at around 60-70 degrees. Once your bow is initiated, stand up on your footpegs, backsweep lightly across your bow with the backside of your paddle and keep your boat on edge by continuing to pull up with your left knee. Keeping your boat on edge and standing up on the footpegs tends to stall the cartwheel long enough for your backsweep to pirouette your kayak 180 degrees. Once your boat has spun 180 degrees, you're ready to initiate your stern and to begin cartwheeling in the opposite direction. Lead the way with your head and body (look over your left shoulder and lean into the next end a bit) and continue to pull up with your left knee to keep your boat tilted to the right. Meanwhile, your back sweep turns into a forward sweep and pulls your stern underwater. Leading with the body usually requires leaning back to initiate the stern, but make sure you get your weight forward again as soon as possible. This sets your body up for the next end of your cartwheel sequence.

Like many vertical moves, the split can be effectively practiced on flatwater. As long as you can cartwheel on flatwater, there's no reason why you can't splitwheel. In some ways the splitwheel is actually easier than the standard cartwheel because you keep an active blade in the water the whole time, and you don't need to make an edge transition. Whether you're practicing in a hole or on the flats,

The splitwheel involves keeping your weight on the same edge, looking over the same shoulder and keeping the same blade in the water.

it will be easiest to initiate the split from your first end. Once you're comfortable with the motions, you can start thinking about splitting-it-up in the middle of a cartwheel sequence. At that point, you're ready for the Tricky Whu... but that's another story.

Overview - Splitwheel

- *After initiating a cartwheel, stand up on your footpegs, backsweep lightly across your bow with the backside of your paddle and keep your boat on edge*
- *After pirouetting 180 degrees, lead with your head and body, and turn your back sweep into a forward sweep.*
- *After initiating the stern, get your weight forward as quickly as possible.*
- *The same blade stays in the water throughout the move.*

Clean / Super Clean Cartwheels

The clean cartwheel is a two-ended cartwheel accomplished with only a single stroke. The super clean cartwheel is a three-ended cartwheel done with only a single stroke. If you were in a freestyle competition, all these ends would need to be at least 45 degrees to make the move count. Though these are the only named 'clean' cartwheels, there is really no limit to how many 'clean' ends you can do. With that said though, cleaning a cartwheel is an advanced move that requires a high level of control when vertical. Nailing one clean end is tricky, never mind 5 clean ends! The best place to practice is on flatwater, but whether you're on the flats, or in a hole, the techniques you'll use won't change.

The key to the clean-wheel is making smooth and efficient edge transitions that let you maintain as much spin momentum as possible. We've been over the concept of maintaining spin momentum many times already, so you should understand that the trick is to avoid 'hitting the wall' by making an early transition to your next edge.

We'll start by considering a clean stern-end of a cartwheel, as it is easier than a bow-clean. Your clean-wheel begins as a regular cartwheel, but after pulling your bow down with a back sweep, you won't be using a forward sweep to help pull your stern through. To compensate for this lack of paddle power, you need to carry through as much spin momentum as possible from your first end, and you need to get your body as active as possible. The way you'll do this is by throwing your body into the move as you make the transition from one edge to the other. This means turning your head and upper body aggressively to lead the spin, while shifting your weight back to help sink the stern. You should be leading so aggressively with your head and body that out of the corner of your eye you can watch your stern enter the water. As soon as your stern does enter the water, you already need to be thinking about your next edge transition, which will need to be made earlier than for a normal cartwheel since you don't have a stroke pulling your stern underwater. To make this edge transition, you'll need to shift your weight from one hip to the next and pull your trailing knee towards your chest. Pulling your knee up not only initiates your edge transition, but it also pulls your body into a forward position which is essential for the continuation of your cartwheel sequence. If you make this transition too early, your cartwheel will flatten out. If you make the transition too late, you will

Kevin's clean cartwheel.

lose your spin momentum (hit the wall), stall, and fall upside down. If you make the transition at the right time, your bow will continue on its path and drop towards the water once again. With your bow falling to the water, keep your head and body turned aggressively into the spin and either plant a back sweep around your hip to re-establish control, or throw your bow down without a stroke for a complete super clean cartwheel. At no point during this move should your boat stall out.

The bow clean tends to be more difficult than the stern clean, whether it is attempted on its own, or as the second part of a super clean cartwheel. This is because the bows of kayaks are bigger than

Instead of planting the second stroke, turn and lead ultra-aggressively with head and body.

As soon as your stern is initiated, pull the trailing knee up and throw your weight onto your other edge. Note that the body is forward before the next stroke is planted.

the sterns, as they need to accommodate our legs, making them more prone to hitting the wall. This means you'll have less room for error, and can't be quite as aggressive with your edging. Otherwise, the concept is the same: you need to pre-establish as much spin momentum as possible from your first end, which involves making a smooth and efficient edge transition. Setting up for your bow clean, you'll be coming around from the stern-end of a cartwheel. Whether it's a clean stern-end or not, you can prepare yourself for the bow clean by keeping your weight back slightly longer than normal as your stern slices through the water. This allows you to throw your weight forward more aggressively when you're ready to initiate the bow. When this time comes, you'll throw your weight forward while at the same time turning your head and upper body to lead the way. As soon as your bow enters the water, you need to be ready for

The body stays back as weight begins to shift from right edge to left.

The body is thrown forward to help initiate the bow.

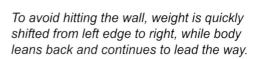

To avoid hitting the wall, weight is quickly shifted from left edge to right, while body leans back and continues to lead the way.

your next edge transition, which involves lifting your leading knee, pushing your trailing knee away from your body, and shifting your weight onto the other hip. As was already mentioned, this transition will need to happen earlier than it did for your stern clean, as the added volume in your bow will prevent you from being as aggressive.

The clean cartwheel is an advanced playboating move that requires great edge control, fantastic balance, and total commitment with your upper body. It relies largely on pre-established spin momentum, along with the power that you can harness from your torso rotation. To get the most out of your torso rotation, think of your body as an elastic band. The more you wind it up, the more power you'll have to use. Commit with your mind and body, and expect to flip learning this move!

Tyler being cleaned.

Overview - Clean / Super Clean Cartwheel

- *The power for the clean comes from pre-established spin momentum, torso rotation, and throwing your body weight into the move.*
- *As soon as your clean end is initiated, prepare to make your edge transition.*
- *Don't try and get your kayak too vertical*

LOOPS

The loop is an advanced playboating move that has been around for a number of years, but it was only in the past year that the loop was refined into one of the most dynamic and impressive moves out there. So what is the loop? The loop is a complete front or back flip. The best loops are actually completely airborne and are amazing to watch. It will probably come as no surprise that boat designs are largely responsible for making this move a reality. Without the right boat, the loop is much more difficult, and getting airborne is only a dream. The best playboats for loops are the short and stubby ones that have the most volume.

Front Loop

The loop actually evolved from a classic playboating move that paddlers have been doing for decades: the ender. Like the good old ender, you'll need a river feature that allows you to drive your bow underwater, while pointing perfectly upstream. Holes, or breaking waves are usually best for this. Once underwater, your kayak will want to get back to the surface as quickly as possible. This is what provides the pop for both the ender, and the loop. With the short boats of today, you'll often need to coax the bow of your kayak underwater by leaning forward. This also helps you to dive more deeply for added pop back out of the water. Now, as soon as your bow has entered the water, it will be taken downstream by the main current, which will bring your kayak vertical. As your bow is taken downstream you must lean right back and stand up on your foot pegs. When your kayak reaches vertical, you should be lying right on the back deck of your kayak. As your kayak passes vertical, it is time to initiate the front flip. This is done in two ways: by jumping up off your foot pegs and throwing your weight aggressively upstream and all the way forward. If you got a good pop out of your initiation you'll be able to do a complete flip and land on your back in the foam pile. Think about this part of the loop like a basketball jump shot. Timing is everything! A good jump shot is taken as the player reaches the height of his jump. Likewise, a loop should be initiated as you reach the top of your pop. If you've set up the loop correctly, your kayak will reach the height of its pop after it has passed vertical. Making this happen consistently will require you to fine-tune the speed that you lean back once your bow has been driven underwater.

As the boat gets taken vertical, lean right back. At the top of the pop, just as your kayak passes vertical, initiate the front flip by jumping off the footpegs and throwing the body upstream and forward.

If all has gone well you should be landing on your back in the foam pile as your stern hits the water. If you've thrown yourself upstream far enough, your stern will hit the greenwater and get pulled downstream, bringing your bow over your head until you're pointing upstream once again. You can help push your bow over your head by leaning back and pushing your feet upstream. Your paddle can also help by grabbing water as quickly and from as far downstream as you can. We could look at this part of the loop in more detail, but the reality is that it happens very quickly and it should be quite natural. The most important part of the move is the initiation of your flip as you reach the peak of your pop. So how is your ender feeling these days anyway?

If the front flip was timed well your stern will land in the greenwater and you'll land flat on your back in the foam pile.

To help your stern pass through, grab water from downstream with your paddle and push your legs upstream.

Overview - Front Loop

- Set up on the foam pile, pointing directly upstream
- *Keeping your boat straight, lean forward to help sink your bow, and then lean back as your kayak is taken vertical.*
- *Initiate the flip by throwing your body forward and upstream as your kayak reaches the top of its pop, which should be after your kayak has passed vertical.*
- *To finish the move, grab water from downstream and push your legs upstream.*

The Back Loop

As you probably guessed, the back loop is simply a front loop done in reverse. What this means is that you'll set up facing downstream and will be initiating your stern. Setting yourself up backward can definitely be a bit tricky, but otherwise, the back loop is no harder than the front loop. Let's look at how it all fits together.

To set up the back loop, you'll want to get on top of the foam pile, with your stern pointed directly upstream and into the stickiest part of the hole. While keeping your boat straight with rudders, you need to dive your stern underwater so you'll pop into the air. Being lower in volume than the bow, your stern will dive more easily and you won't get as much pop from it. This means that you won't need to coax the stern underwater as much as you did the bow, so you can stay sitting upright. If you do need to give the stern a little help, lean back slightly until it catches. Once caught, you need to get your weight forward quickly so that your knees are pulled right into your chest by the time your kayak reaches vertical. Just as with the front loop, the idea is to have your kayak reach the top of its pop just after your kayak passes vertical. At this point, you'll initiate the back flip by throwing your weight right onto your back deck and pulling your knees hard against the thigh braces to bring your bow over top your body. You should be able to land face and chest first in the foam pile as your bow hits the greenwater. The greenwater will now pull your bow under your body and finish your back loop. You can help out with this last stage by continuing to pull your knees toward your chest and by pushing downward and downstream with your paddle blades. Though it is awkward to get a powerful stroke from this position, any push you can get from your paddle will be helpful.

Lean forward as the kayak is taken vertical. At the top of your pop, when your kayak has just passed vertical, throw your body right back and pull the bow down with your knees.

Overview - Back Loop

- *Set up on the foam pile facing downstream, with your stern pointed directly upstream.*
- *Keeping your boat straight, dive your stern underwater, and then lean forward as your kayak is taken vertical.*
- *Initiate the back flip by throwing your body right on your back deck as your kayak reaches the top of its pop, which should be after your kayak has passed vertical.*
- *Landing on your face and chest, pull your knees to your chest and push down and away with your paddle to finish the move.*

Space Godzilla

The space Godzilla was once referred to as the 'modified loop'

because of the similarities between the two moves. You'll set up and initiate the space Godzilla the same way as you did for the front loop. The loop gets modified when your kayak passes vertical and you throw yourself into a front tuck. Instead of just throwing yourself directly forward, you'll actually tuck forward and to one side. This will cause your kayak to rotate as it flips over top your body, so your stern will hit the water on edge, as it would for a cartwheel. Your stern will then slice through the water like a super fast cartwheel. The result of the cartwheel will depend on what angle your stern slices through the water and, as you might guess, this will take lots of practice to control.

Corran going aerial

Tricky Whu - by Tyler Curtis

The tricky whu is another great example of a move that happened by accident the first time. Though I'm sure it had happened to others before me, I'll never forget my first, completely unintentional tricky whu. It was at the end of the summer of 2000, during the finals for the Ottawa River Rodeo. It was a loaded finals, with EJ, Wick, Shane Benedict, Ken Whiting, Kevin Varette, and many others. Everyone was having great rides, but I still felt that it was my competition to win. I was at the top of my game and I absolutely loved the hole. With one last ride to win the title, I dropped in and threw down as hard as I possible could. It paid off. I had going one of my best rides ever, and with only 10 seconds left I went for a big splitwheel. When I came around, I caught my stern edge in a funny way, did a full pirouette right back into the hole, and went right back into cartwheels. The crowd went nuts and I walked away with the winner's trophy. In the days that followed, my buddies and I talked about that 'nameless' move all the time. There had to be a way of controlling it! After hours of sinus flushing, we finally made the breakthrough and the 'matrix' was born. A few months later, the matrix evolved into the tricky whu, which is now one of the coolest moves you'll see on the river.

So how does the tricky whu work? The tricky whu is basically a splitwheel linked right into a stern pirouette. The move uses a single paddle blade and requires great balance (stomach muscles) and edge control (upper/lower body separation). Let's look at the tricky whu from the very beginning.

The tricky whu will work best in relatively powerful holes. The move starts with the initiation of a cartwheel on the bow. As the stern reaches vertical it is time to split-it-up and initiate the stern end in the opposite direction. (If you haven't already sorted out your splitwheel, then you might as well go back and work on it, because this is the easiest part of the move!) For the tricky whu, you'll want to pirouette your splitwheel a bit more than you might normally. This will cause your stern to initiate, with greenwater hitting the deck of your stern rather than the hull of your stern. This greenwater will give your stern pirouette a boost. As soon as this stern end is initiated, the second part of the trick comes in. You now want your kayak to stern pirouette (180 degree rotation) around that same paddle blade that you have kept planted in the water. At this point, three things need to happen: 1. the blade that was used to initiate the stern turns into

an open face draw and starts pulling your bow around, 2. your head and body turn, leading the pirouette, and 3. you keep your weight balanced on the same edge. Because the greenwater is grabbing your stern, all of these things will have to happen quickly in order for you to avoid landing on your head.

By over-rotating your splitwheel, the main current will catch the deck of your stern, and help pirouette you around.

Before reaching vertical, the forward sweep that initiated the stern becomes an open faced bow draw.

With weight kept over the left edge of the boat, the bow draw pulls the bow around while the head and body lead the way.

Once your bow comes around to point upstream again, roll your paddle into a low-brace/backstroke and slam the bow of your kayak back into an end. Keeping your weight forward during the pirouette will help you stay balanced and will help prevent you from falling past vertical. It also makes it easier to roll your blade over for the smash (backstroke) needed to continue cartwheeling.

The most common mistake is allowing the stern to flatten out on the split, rather than slicing the stern into the water. If your stern catches like this, you'll end up doing a back ender instead of a stern pirouette.

Billy Harris: The commitment of the Tricky Whu.

Overview - Tricky Whu

- *Initiate a standard splitwheel, but pirouette your splitwheel a touch more than normal.*
- *When your stern is initiated, turn your paddle into an open-face bow draw, lead with your head and change edges.*
- *When your bow has come around, turn your paddle into a backstroke and pull the bow down.*
- *Keep your weight forward throughout the move.*

Tyler kick flipping on the Futaleufu.

River Moves

SPLATS

Once a move exclusive to squirt boats, the splat has become a common river running move for freestyle paddlers as it's a great way to liven up a mellow section of whitewater. A splat is a vertical bow, or stern stall that is done against the upstream face of a rock, in which your boat is kept between yourself and the rock.

First, you need to learn to recognize a good splat rock (one that's deep enough, and isn't undercut!). If you can't reliably pick out a good splat rock while on the fly, then take the time to thoroughly scout the area. Splatting the wrong rock can really ruin your day! The ideal splat rock is an almost-vertical, rounded rock with mellow current flowing into it, forming a stable, but not an overly big pillow. A pillow is the cushion of water that is formed when current runs into something immovable. For the most part, pillows are paddler-friendly features as they indicate that an object is not undercut. Aside from the pillow, you'll also want it to be relatively deep along the sides of the rock where you'll be exiting from your splat.

The Stern Splat

The stern splat involves sinking the stern of your kayak and lifting your bow into the air. You can establish a stern splat in two ways: you can either stern squirt, or sweep your bow into the air. Sweeping the bow into the air tends to be easiest and involves using a well-timed stern pivot turn. Approach the rock from directly upstream, floating at around a 45 degree angle. When you're close enough to lift your bow onto the face of the rock, initiate your stern pivot turn by taking a powerful sweep on the upstream side of your kayak, with your boat tilted into the sweep. The idea is to time your pivot turn so that your bow lands on the rock face when your kayak has spun to 6 o'clock. The main current will then help push your stern more vertical until the pillow coming off the rock stalls you.

You can also stern squirt your boat into a splat. Again the idea is to time your stern squirt so that your bow lands on the face of the rock when your kayak is pointing directly downstream (6 o'clock). This stern squirt entry involves floating into the splat rock almost sideways rather than at 45 degrees. When the time has come to initiate your stern squirt, you'll be using a back sweep on the downstream side of your kayak, with your boat tilted away from the sweep.

Float towards the rock at around a 45 degree angle

Initiate an aggressive stern pivot turn.

As your kayak reaches 6 o'clock the bow lands on the rock.

Both the stern squirt and sweeping methods of establishing a splat are very committing as they involve initiating your upstream edge. To avoid flipping upstream, you'll have to dig in deeply with your paddle blade and initiate the move quickly and powerfully. Once your bow is up on the rock, there are a few tricks for keeping yourself in the splat. First of all, you need to have an active blade in the water at all possible times. Secondly, there's a common misconception about the different forward and backward leans that you'll use when your kayak is on end. Believe it or not, if you want to bring your stern splat more vertical, you should lean forward. If you want to stop yourself from going over vertical, you should lean back! This goes against most people's natural instincts, but think about it this way. When you lean back, you're actually pushing your legs away from you. When you lean forward, you're pulling your legs (bow) towards your chest. With this said, you can expect to have to adjust your body leans to deal with different situations, but ultimately, your body should be in a relatively neutral position, which tends to work the stomach muscles.

The Bow Splat

The bow splat is a bow stall against a rock face. This move is a bit more advanced than the stern splat because it is harder to know your position on the rock, as you will be facing down and upstream. The best way of establishing a bow splat is by approaching the rock from upstream, floating almost sideways, then throwing your bow down just before the seam of the pillow, using the standard double pump technique. Of course you'll want to do this in the direction that will keep your kayak in between you and the rock. Because the

Overview - Stern Splat

- *Learn to recognize a good splat rock (one that isn't undercut, and is deep on the upstream side, and along the sides)*
- *Whether stern squirting or sweeping your bow into the air, timing is the key. Your bow needs to land on the face of the rock when your kayak is pointing directly downstream (6 o'clock).*
- *Keep an active blade in the water.*
- *Leaning forward takes you more vertical, while leaning back flattens out your kayak.*
- *Keep your kayak between you and the rock!*

current will be helping to push your kayak vertical, throw your bow down at a slightly lower angle than you would throw it down for a flatwater cartwheel. Like the stern splat, timing is key, as you need your stern to land on the face of the rock with your kayak pointing directly upstream. You'll then have to stop your kayak at 12 o'clock with a braking stroke. You'll then stabilize your bow stall by getting both your paddle blades in the water, which sets up your 'tripod' (if you haven't already reviewed the 'Bow Stall' segment, this would be a good time). In most cases, you'll need to make small adjustments to maintain this bow splat. As we discussed in the 'Bow Stall' segment, the forward and backward leans that you'll use when balancing on your bow, are often confused. Leaning forward will bring your legs to your chest and flatten out your kayak. Leaning back will bring your boat more vertical as you push your bow down and away from your body. This means that if you find yourself falling over vertical when bow splatting, then you should lean forward more aggressively.

Initiate your bow at the seam of the pillow on a slightly lower angle than you would on flatwater.

Stop your boat at vertical, then stabilize your stall by getting both blades in the water. Keep your weight forward.

Exiting from a splat isn't usually a concern, as the main current will pull you around the sides of the rock. If you flip against the splat rock, there's no graceful way to recover. You can try to roll up on your downstream side, against the rock, but there often isn't enough room for your paddle. This means you'll have to roll on your upstream side, which is considerably more difficult. If you don't make it up on this side, you should at least be able to get a quick breath so that you can comfortably hang out upside down until you are face-surfed past the splat rock. This scenario gives you a good reason for being picky about the splat rocks you choose. Trust me when I say that it only takes one knuckle scraping to appreciate a splat rock with a large recovery zone!

Overview - Bow Splat

- *Float sideways into the splat rock, and initiate with a low angle double pump, just before the seam of the pillow.*
- *Time your bow initiation so that your stern lands on the rock with your kayak pointed to 12 o'clock.*
- *Once vertical, put on the brakes, and get established in a bow stall, with both paddle blades in the water.*
- *When in a bow splat, leaning forward flattens out your kayak and leaning back takes you more vertical.*

My favorite... The body splat. Putting Billy in his place!

Splatwheels

A splatwheel is simply a cartwheel done along the face of a rock. I won't go into the specifics for the splatwheel because we already covered all the skills necessary in the flatwater cartwheeling segment. The only difference is that you have a pillow to deal with. The only piece of advice that I can offer is to initiate each end at a slightly lower angle than you would on flatwater, as the current will be helping to push your kayak vertical. If you initiate your ends too vertically, you'll find yourself passing vertical and flopping onto your face.

ROCK SPINS

The rock 360 is a full spin accomplished with your kayak perched on top of a rock. If you don't mind scratching up the bottom of your kayak, then this is one of the best ways to spice up mellow sections of river. If you don't like scraping up the bottom of your kayak… then borrow someone else's boat.

First, you need to find a smooth, rounded rock, with current running into it, and with fairly deep water surrounding it. Once you've found your rock, the challenge is driving yourself into a balanced position on top of the rock. It requires a soft touch to competently run yourself up onto a rock, far enough to prevent your upstream edge from catching, but not so far that you'll slide off its backside. Once you can do this reliably, you're ready to add the spin.

You need to decide beforehand which way you're going to spin. In general, you'll want to spin your bow away from the strongest current. This tends to get the water working for you. Taking a situation where the strongest current is on the river right side of a rock, you'll drive yourself onto the rock, and then spin your bow to the left. The reason you need to make this decision beforehand is that your last stroke (which drives you onto the rock) should give your kayak spin momentum in the direction that you want to spin. In this situation, you'll want your last stroke to be a forward sweep stroke on the right, which starts turning your kayak to the left as you climb onto the rock. Once on top, you'll initiate the rock 360 in much the same way that you initiate a stern squirt. You'll rotate your body aggressively into the spin (to the left in this case), and reach as far to your stern as you can to plant a back sweep/pivot at the back of the boat. You should be able to see our paddle enter the water at the stern of your kayak. Unlike the stern squirt, you need to keep your boat flat as you push on the back sweep and pull your bow around. Ideally, you've rotated so much that you can plant your back sweep/pivot in the water that rushes to the right of the rock. You'll then get an incredible amount of power from your backstroke. Now that your kayak is spinning, you should be able to do a full 360 by leading with your head. If you've balanced yourself well enough on the rock, you can even do multiple spins by continuing to take pivot/sweep strokes while pulling the bow around with your knees and stomach muscles. As when linking cartwheels or flat spins, once your boat is spinning it becomes less important to reach for your strokes, and more important to get your next paddle in the water right away. You can then maintain your spin momentum more effectively. This means you'll drop your next blade into the water between your hip and knee rather than reaching to your toes. As always you'll continue to lead the way with your head and upper body. Before you know it, you'll be doing rock 720's!

With the main current passing to the river right of the rock, you'll spin your bow to the left. Note how aggressively the body rotates to plant the back sweep at the stern, and that the head leads the way at all times.

Overview - Rock 360

- *Choose a smooth, rounded rock with current hitting it.*
- *Spin in the direction that sweeps your bow away from the fastest current.*
- *Establish spin momentum with your last stroke.*
- *Once on the rock, initiate the rock 360 with an aggressive back sweep.*
- *When linking rock spins, get your following strokes in the water as quickly as possible.*

WAVE WHEELS

The wave wheel is an airborne cartwheel that is done while launching off the peak of a standing wave. Freestyle paddlers sometimes use it as an entry move into a hole, but more often than not, the wave wheel is a means of spicing up a wave train. The bigger the wave you choose to use, the more dynamic your wave wheel will be. With a big enough wave you can even get your whole kayak out of the water! Learning to fly this way is remarkably easy once you've figured out the flatwater cartwheel. The trickiest part will then be lining up your approach and timing your initiation stroke.

So what's the best type of wave for wave wheels? The best waves are relatively steep (but not breaking) and deep on their backside. Trust me when I say that it only takes one wave wheel into shallow water to make you appreciate how important it is to have a deep wave!

To line up a wave wheel, you'll want speed, but your focus should be on taking a final, powerful launching stroke on the face of the wave, just before you reach the wave's peak. This launching stroke is used to do two things: it pulls your bow into the air, and pulls your hip past the wave's peak. To do both these things, the launching stroke is a cross between a power stroke and the double pump. Here's how it works. As you climb the face of a wave, tilt your kayak right on edge and plant the launching stroke at your toes with your top hand at shoulder level. This stroke will pull down on the water to lift your bow and forward to launch you from the wave.

The launching stroke pulls the bow into the air and the hip past the peak of the wave.

As soon as this stroke finishes, continue with the standard flatwater cartwheel motions: rotate your head and shoulders aggressively downwards and turn your launching stroke into a back/pivot stroke planted near the back of your boat and at the peak of the wave. With your body wound up and your backstroke planted, you'll throw your weight forward, push your stern into the air, and pull your bow down aggressively with your stomach and knees. After hitting your first end, you can keep the wave wheel going using your flatwater cartwheeling technique in coordination with the bobbing action of your boat. When you nail the wave wheel, your bow will pencil into the trough of the next wave, and then pop back out. This pop will give your subsequent ends a great boost. If you've got a continuous wave train to work with, it will also help to initiate your following ends as you reach the peak of the next wave. By using the pop of your boat and the peaks of the following waves, you can establish a neat bobbing, cartwheel rhythm.

When your hip passes the peak of the wave your body should be facing downward. Push off your back stroke, pull your bow downward, and throw your weight forward in standard flatwater cartwheel fashion.

Having nailed the first end of the wave wheel, the kayak pencils into the trough of the next wave. Ideally, the next end of the wave wheel is initiated as the boat pops back out of the water, and as you reach the peak of the next wave.

Overview - Wave Wheel

- *Choose a steep, deep wave and hit it straight-on with speed.*
- *Take a launching stroke that pulls your bow into the air, and your hip past the peak of the wave.*
- *Turn your launching stroke into a back/pivot stroke at the peak of the wave, and throw your bow down in flatwater cartwheel fashion: leading aggressively with head and body, throwing your weight forward and pulling with your stomach and knees.*
- *Keep your wave wheel going by initiating subsequent ends at the peaks of the following waves.*

KICK FLIPS

The kick flip is basically an airborne, horizontal pirouette that is done when launching off a wave. This has always been one of my favourite moves! In fact, I'll never forget the first time I saw someone do a kick flip. It was about 8 years ago at the bottom of McKoy's, on the Ottawa River. At the time the move had no name and I didn't know that it existed. A French slalom paddler came flying downstream, hit a big wave and corkscrewed in the air. My buddies and I couldn't believe what we'd seen! Of course we hiked up and tried it ourselves, but had no luck. It wasn't long until the move became somewhat of an old wive's tale, as the move hadn't been seen since then. A year or so later, I started thinking about that move again. Boats had changed a great deal since that time, so I knew that a different approach had to be taken. Since I couldn't get the same speed that that slalom boater had, I would need a steeper wave… I wish I could describe the shock that ran through my body when I nailed that first one.

So what can I tell you about the kick flip? First of all, in order to nail a kick flip, you'll need a very steep wave, plenty of speed and total body and mind commitment! You'll also need to have developed the skills necessary for throwing advanced play moves like the flatwater cartwheel. Let's now break down the move into its set-up, initiation, and recovery.

The kick flip is set up in exactly the same way as the wave wheel. You'll need plenty of downstream speed directed towards the steepest part of a wave, but the timing of your last / launching stroke is the most important thing. This last stroke gets taken as you ride up the face of the wave, with your boat rolling up on edge. As you pull the launching stroke through, thrust your hips forward and roll your kayak further

As the launching stroke pulls through, the body commits to the move.

and further on edge. The goal here is to launch yourself from the wave and to pull your bow into the air. As you finish the stroke, lean right back, turn your body aggressively into the pirouette and plant the backside of your active blade behind, and underneath your boat. Your paddle should now be in a powerful low brace position, from which you forcefully push your stern over your head and body. At this same time, throw your head, top hand and body into the pirouette. With a good launching stroke, a powerful push off, and your head and body leading the way, you should be able to do a complete pirouette. Nailing a kick flip means landing flat on the water with a smack. If

Lying right back, and with the head and body leading the way, the launching stroke turns into a low brace planted under the stern, from which the stern gets pushed over the head.

With a good launch and a powerful push off your low brace, you can do a completely airborne pirouette.

you don't get your kayak completely around, there's a good chance you'll land on a high brace. It's tempting to force the move through, but this can put serious strain on your shoulders. Instead, keep your arms in close to your body and swing yourself forward, with your wrists cocked back so that your paddle is on a sculling angle. This sculling blade will provide the purchase from which you can roll your boat upright. This may not be as quick as using a monster brace, but it can save you a whole lot of pain!

Commitment is the name of the game for the kick flip.

Overview - Kick Flip

- *Choose a steep, green wave, and hit it with speed, focusing on a well-timed launching stroke.*
- *Roll your kayak further and further on edge as you pull on your launching stroke. Commit!*
- *Lean right back, plant a low brace under your kayak, then push off your paddle and snap your hips, bringing your kayak over top your body*
- *Be careful not to land on a big high brace.*

Mystery Move

Squirt boats have played a major role in the development of freestyle kayaking. In fact, one could easily make the argument that today's playboats are simply plastic squirt boats. But until a playboat can corkscrew its way down on an eddyline and mystery its way into the underworld, the squirt boat will remain in a class of its own. For those not familiar with the term 'mystery move', the mystery involves completely sinking the boat, body and paddle, and no, it has nothing to do with popping your skirt. As I mentioned, squirt boats can corkscrew down on an eddyline by use of the conflicting currents. Playboats don't have this same ability because of their extra volume, and so to mystery, they need actual downward moving currents. We'll find these currents in pour-overs. So, here's how it works.

First of all, use your common sense when choosing a pour-over to try this on. If it isn't deep and friendly, then stay away from it. The idea is to stick your bow and stern in the greenwater so that you get pulled down, under the foam pile. Since your bow has more volume than your stern, you'll initiate it first. Approach the pour-over from below with a bit of speed. You don't need to charge overly hard into it, but you can't be moving too slowly either, as your ends won't catch enough greenwater. You'll want to enter on a strong lateral angle, but not quite sideways, and your boat should be held flat. When your bow catches, your upstream edge will be pulled down forcefully, so make sure you're prepared for this by shifting your weight over your downstream edge. If you're not ready, you'll do the most impressive wathunk imaginable. As your bow catches and your upstream edge gets pulled down, slice your stern down into the greenwater by leaning back slightly and taking a snappy back sweep on the downstream side. As your stern is thrown down, you need to flatten out your kayak and bring your body back to an aggressive forward position. The whole length of your kayak should now be in the greenwater, being pulled downward. Your paddle will usually end up above your head like a helicopter rotor, and will be useful as a brace to keep your boat level. Now all you can do is enjoy the ride.

If you've ever tapped into the underworld, then you'll understand when I say that this has to be one of the coolest feelings in the world. If you haven't yet done so, then this move will be a treat once you figure it out. It really gives you an appreciation for the power of the

Plow your bow into the greenwater with your kayak on a strong lateral angle, and your weight on your downstream edge.

river. It almost feels as though you're hitching a ride on a freight train that is the moving water. You can't fight it. All you can do is go with the flow. Of course this means that if you mistime your entry onto the train, things will quickly go sour. You're either on it, or you're not! The trickiest part of this move is the timing of sinking your stern after your bow engages, and then levelling off your boat. There is a very fine line for success. Expect to get tossed around when learning this, so if you have any compassion for your sinuses, use nose plugs.

Overview - Mystery

- *Enter a friendly pour-over from downstream with speed and on a strong lateral angle.*
- *As your bow catches, shift your weight onto your downstream edge and slice your stern down into the greenwater with a snappy back sweep.*
- *When your stern is level with your bow, flatten your boat.*

presents

The Playboater's Destination Checklist

Country	Playspot	Type	Time of Year
Australia	Penrith Stadium	Multiple Features	All year
	NSW, Goolang Creek	Playhole	All year
Austria	River Isel, Dolomite Wave	Breaking Wave	May-Sept
	River Inn, Ried Wave	Breaking Wave	May-Sept
	River Saalach, Lofer	Playhole	May-July
Belgium	River Ourthe, Tillf	Playhole	Low Water
	River Ourthe, Tron-Chique	Breaking Waves	Nov-March
	River Ourthe, Barvaux	Breaking Wave	Nov-March
Canada	Skookumchuk, BC	Tidal Rapid	April-Nov
	Lachine Rapids, Montreal	Waves	May-Oct
	Sturgeon Falls, Winnipeg	Waves and holes	May – Oct
	Reversing Falls, Saint John	Tidal Rapid	June – Oct
	Slave River, NWT	Waves	June-Sept
	Ottawa River	Waves and Holes	April-Oct
Chile	Rio Futaleufu, Terminator Wave	Wave	Jan-April
	Rio San Pedro, Pucone	Wave and holes	Dec-April
Costa Rica	Talamanca, Grape Point	Ocean Surfing	All year
Czech Republic	River Moldau, Veltrusy	Multiple Features	High Water
	River Moldau, Troja	Multiple Features	All year
Germany	River Luhe, Luhe Walze	Playhole	May-Sept
	River Isar, Plattling	Wave/Hole	April-Nov
	Augsburg, Eiskanal	Multiple Features	All Year
Finland	Lieska, Neitikoski	Wave/Hole	May-Sept
France	River Cher, St Aignan	Breaking Wave	Nov-April
	River Rhone, Hawaii Sur Rhone	Wave/Hole	June-Sept
	River Durance, Rabioux	Breaking Wave	June-Sept
Holland	River Roer, Roermond Steps	Multiple Features	All Year
	North Sea, Bergen ann Zee	Ocean Surfing	March-Oct

Country	Playspot	Type	Time of Year
Iceland	Lagarflot, Lagarfloss Weir	Wave/Hole	May-Aug
Ireland	River Liffey, The Sluice	Playhole	High Water
Italy	Dora Baltea, Villeneuve	Wave/Hole	June-Aug
	Canale Naviglio Grande, Turbo	Breaking Wave	June-Sept
	River Mis, Mis Hole	Breaking Wave	March-Sept
Japan	Tamagawa river, Obonai wave	Breaking Wave	Nov-March
Norway	Vosso, Bulken Wave	Breaking Wave	High Water
	River Sjoa, Faukstad	Playhole	May-Aug
	River Otta, Skjåk (The Hole)	Wave/Hole	May-Aug
New Zealand	Kaituna River, Kaituna Hole	Playhole	All Year
	Waikato River, Full James	Breaking Wave	All Year
Russia	St Petersburg, Porog Bolshoi Toll	Playhole	April-July
Slovakia	River Danube, Cunovo Centre	Multiple Features	All Year
Slovenia	River Soca, Soca Hole	Playhole	March-Sept
South Africa	Vaal River, Gatsien Wave	Breaking Wave,	Oct-March
Spain	Carasa River, Ola de Carasa	Tidal Feature	Tidal
	Noguera Pallaresa River, Sort	Playhole	March-Sept
	River Miño, Miño wave	Breaking Wave	March-Sept
Sweden	River Ljusnan, Hovrahällarna	Wave/Hole	March-Sept
Switzerland	River Reuss, Bremgarten	Wave/Hole	May-Aug
	River Aare, Thun	Breaking Wave	March-Sept
	River Vorderrhein, Surf City	Wave/Hole	June-Aug
UK	River Trent, Holme PierrePont	Multiple Features	All Year
	River Thames, Hurley Weir	Wave/Hole	Nov-March
	River Tryweryn, WW Course	Multiple Features	All Year

Country	Playspot	Type	Time of Year
USA	Rock Island, Tennessee	Hole	All Year
	Payette River	Hole	Spring
	Gauley River	Holes and Waves	All Year
	Deschutes River, Tressle	Wave	Jan-April
	Black River, Hole Brothers	Hole	All Year
	Ocoee River, Hell Hole	Hole	All Year
Zambia	The Zambezi	Multiple Features	July-Jan

Terminator wave, Rio Futaleufu, Chile

Where are we going to go this weekend? Probably the most asked question in the history of kayaking - and the answer can be found on Playak.com. This independent, volunteer-driven site provides everything that the playboating junkie requires to plan a road trip. Visit playak.com for full details on the best playboating destinations in the world, including directions, photos and details about the locations.

Glossary

6 o'clock: pointing directly downstream.

12 o'clock: pointing directly upstream.

Aerial: a move that involves getting the complete boat and body out of the water.

Backdeck roll: a quick roll that involves leaning right on the back deck of the kayak.

Backside (of a wave): the part of a wave downstream of the peak, where water flows downhill.

Backside (of a paddle): the convex side of the paddle blade

Backstab: a reverse blunt

Back surfing: using gravity to maintain a position on the face of a wave in which your kayak is facing downstream.

Blast: front surfing in the trough of a hole, with the stern under the foam pile.

Blunt: an aggressive spin from front surf to back surf that throws the stern into the air.

Boat tilt: the balancing of your weight on a single butt cheek or hip, which leans your boat on edge.

Body wind-up: the rotation of your upper body in the desired turning direction.

Boil line: the point on a hole's foam pile at which the water on the upstream side flows upstream, while the water on the downstream side flows downstream.

Bow: the front end of a kayak.

Bow wind-up: the pulling of the bow into the air in order to achieve more energy with which to throw it downwards.

Brake: a surfing stroke that causes maximum resistance with the main current, used to pull the surfer downstream on the wave.

Cartwheel: a standard, advanced playboating move done on flatwater and in holes, in which the bow and stern rotate around the body, staying 45 degrees or more past horizontal.

Clean: a move that involves a full 360-degree rotation with only a single stroke.

Corner: the side of a hole that can be used for spinning, setting up advanced moves, or exiting.

Cross bow draw: a forward sweep stroke planted with the front arm completely crossing the bow of the kayak.

Deck: the top of the kayak

Downstream: the direction in which the water is flowing.

Double pump: the action of winding up the bow.

Eddyline: the line of turbulent water separating two currents that are travelling in different directions.

Ender: letting the current take the bow or stern of a kayak underwater so that the boat's buoyancy can pop the boat vertically into the air.

Face (of a wave): the part of a wave upstream of the peak and downstream of the trough, in which water is flowing uphill.

Ferry angle: the angle of a kayak to the current that allows the water to push the kayak laterally.

Flat spin: using a flat hull's planing capabilities to change your kayak's direction on the green part of a wave.

Flatwater: water without current.

Flip turn: a wave move than involves snapping the boat over top the body, then landing back in a front surf.

Foam pile: the aerated, re-circulating water that forms the white part of a hole.

Foot pegs: the foot supports in the bow of a kayak.

Front surf: using gravity to maintain an upstream facing position on the face of a wave.

Greenwater: the non-aerated water that flows into and under a hole.

Kick flip: a horizontal pirouette performed while launching from the peak of a wave.

Helix: an upside down, aerial, 360 spin on a wave.

High brace: a method of preventing a flip by pushing against the water surface with the power face of your paddle.

Hip snap: the action responsible for rolling a boat from one edge to another.

Hole (Hydraulic): a type of wave in which the water piles up on itself, forcing aerated water back upstream and into the trough.

Hull: the bottom of the kayak.

Low brace: a method of preventing a flip by pushing against the water surface with the backside of your paddle.

Loop: an airborne flip, done either forward or backward.

Mystery move: a move that involves using downward flowing current to pull boat and body completely underwater.

Offset: the angle at which a paddle's blades are twisted relative to each other.

Party trick: a move that involves going from upside down to a bow stall.

Peak: the highest point on a wave.

Pillow: the area of still water that is piled against the upstream face of a rock.

Pirouette: spinning a kayak around on its end.

Pivot turn: an efficient change of direction that involves having one end of the kayak underwater and the other in the air.

Planing hull: a flat hull that, when surfing, will rise to the surface and allow a kayak to flat spin.

Playboat: a high performance kayak that is designed for taking advantage of river features.

Power face: the concave side of a paddle blade.

Power stroke: a vertical, or past vertical forward stroke that is designed to have minimal impact on spin momentum.

River left: the left-hand side of the river when looking downstream.

River right: the right-hand side of the river when looking downstream.
Rock 360: a flat spin done while balanced on a rock, with the ends of the kayak out of the water.
Rudder: a blade that is planted in the water to control a front or back surf.

Screw-up: a roll performed when passing vertical in a stern squirt, which starts before the kayak has a chance to land upside down.

Scull: the action of taking strokes with paddle blades angled so that they continuously work their way to the surface.

Seam (of a hole): the point in the trough of a hole at which the foam pile meets the greenwater.

Seam (of a pillow): the line dividing the current that flows into the rock from upstream and the rock's pillow.

Shoulder (of a wave): the sides of a wave.

Side surfing: establishing a balanced position on a single hip in the trough of a hole, while being held perpendicular to the main current by the hole's re-circulating water.

Space Godzilla: an aerial loop with a 90-degree twist.

Splat: a vertical stall against the upstream face of a rock, keeping the kayak between rock and body.

Splatwheel: cartwheels performed along the upstream face of a rock.

Splitwheel: pirouetting the kayak 180 degrees while cartwheeling in order to change the direction of the cartwheels.

Squirt boat: an ultra low volume kayak designed to work with the currents below the surface.

Stall: balancing a kayak on end.

Stern: the back end of the kayak.

Stern squirt: a 360-degree pirouette with the bow in the air that is initiated with a back sweep.

Stern wind-up: the lifting of the stern into the air so as to achieve more energy to throw it downwards.

Super clean: a 540-degree spin accomplished with only a single initiating stroke.

Surfer's left: the left side of the river when looking upstream (from a front surfer's perspective)

Surfer's right: the right side of the river when looking upstream (from a front surfer's perspective)

Surge: a fluctuation in the size of a water feature.

Sweep: a stroke used to turn the kayak.

Tongue: a weak spot in a hole that water flows through freely.

Torso rotation: the turning of your upper body that gets all major muscles involved with strokes rather than just the arms.

Tricky-whu: an advanced move that combines a splitwheel with a stern pirouette.

Trough: the lowest point in a hole.

Upstream: the direction from which water is flowing.

Volume: the amount of water in a river.

Wathunk: an incredibly advanced, high-speed upstream flip in a hole.

Wave: a feature created by water piling up on itself.

Wave train: a series of waves.

Wave wheel: a cartwheel initiated as one launches from the peak of a wave.

Zero to Hero: a flatwater move that involves moving from upside down to a stern stall in one fluid motion.

More Great Books from Fox Chapel Publishing

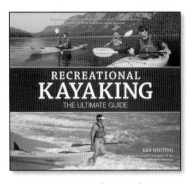

**Recreational Kayaking
The Ultimate Guide**
ISBN: 978-1-56523-640-0 **$19.95**

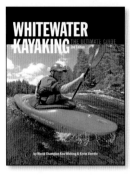

**Whitewater Kayaking The
Ultimate Guide – 2nd Edition**
ISBN: 978-1-896980-73-7 **$29.99**

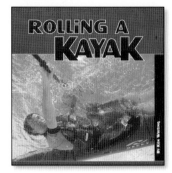

Rolling a Kayak
ISBN: 978-1-56523-645-5 **$16.95**

**Paddling Chef,
Second Edition, The**
ISBN: 978-1-56523-714-8 **$16.95**

Camp Cooking in the Wild
ISBN: 978-1-56523-715-5 **$19.95**

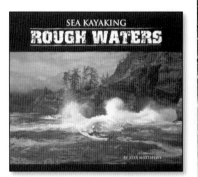

Sea Kayaking Rough Waters
ISBN: 978-1-56523-633-2 **$19.95**

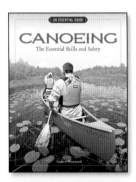

**Canoeing: The Essential
Skills and Safety**
ISBN: 978-1-896980-69-0 **$19.95**

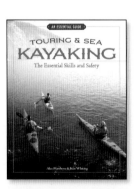

**Touring & Sea Kayaking The
Essential Skills and Safety**
ISBN: 978-1-896980-71-3 **$19.95**

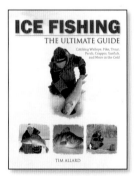

**Ice Fishing: The
Ultimate Guide**
ISBN: 978-1-896980-72-0 **$24.99**

Look for These Books at Your Local Bookstore or Specialty Retailer or at *www.FoxChapelPublishing.com*